MOVING IN GOD'S DIRECTION

MOVING IN GOD'S DIRECTION

Essentials of Christ-centered
Spiritual and Vocational Direction

A guide for spiritual directors, directees, and the spiritually hungry,

including topics worth exploring in the direction session,

plus questions for personal reflection

Mary Sharon Moore

AWAKENING VOCATIONS
Eugene, Oregon

MOVING IN GOD'S DIRECTION

Essentials of Christ-centered Spiritual and Vocational Direction

Awakening Vocations | 4150 Oak Street | Eugene OR 97405

www.awakeningvocations.com

ISBN-13: 978-1479187966 | ISBN-10: 1479187968

Front cover photo: Mary Sharon Moore.

Back cover photo: File photo, Awakening Vocations.

Manufactured in the United States of America on 30% postconsumer waste recycled material; Forest Stewardship Council (FSC)-certified.

CONTENTS

ACKNOWLEDGMENTS

This book came about through the invitation of Kathryn Marcellino of catholicspiritualdirection.com who nudged me to write a series of columns explaining spiritual direction. If a series of columns, why not a book? Thank you, Kathryn!

I owe a debt of gratitude to Francis Kelly Nemeck, OMI, and Marie Theresa Coombs, canonical hermit, of Lebh Shomea House of Prayer in Sarita, Texas, for their deep study and eloquent writings on the fine-tuned workings of the Holy Spirit in the spiritual direction relationship and in the vocation discernment process.

And my own formator in the art and practice of spiritual direction, Antoinette Traeger, OSB, of Queen of Angels Monastery in Mount Angel, Oregon, holds a special place in my heart.

The Lord GOD has given me

   a well-trained tongue,

That I might know how to speak to the weary

   a word that will rouse them.

Morning after morning

   he opens my ear that I may hear;

And I have not rebelled,

   have not turned back.   *Isaiah 50:4–5*[1]

By faith Abraham obeyed when he was called to go out to a place that he was to receive as an inheritance; he went out, not knowing where he was to go. ... For he thought that the one who had made the promise was worthy of his trust.

Hebrews 11:8–11 (author's wording)

There is something I cannot learn alone on my spiritual path, no matter how much I try and no matter how much I want. As I cannot perform an operation on myself, I need the hand of another whom I trust in matters of the soul. A good spiritual director is that "other."   *A directee*

---

[1] Unless otherwise noted, all Scripture references are to the *New American Bible* (Grand Rapids, MI: Catholic World Press, 1987).

INTRODUCTION

What is Christ-centered Spiritual and Vocational Direction?

Perhaps you remember when personal trainers and life coaches were all the buzz. Everyone from celebrities to budding entrepreneurs had their mentor, their coach, their trainer, to whom they tithed their rising fortunes to keep them focused, disciplined, and motivated toward higher goals. Personal trainers became "the new therapists." Spirituality, jettisoned earlier by many in this fast-moving crowd, was now repackaged, rebranded, and "in" again, embraced by these cultural and corporate icons as a way to achieve one's personal best—and perhaps even to dominate one's chosen field.

Connecting the dots to our lives in the twenty-first century, we find it easy to ask: Are today's spiritual directors our culture's "new personal trainers"?

Spiritual directors have been around for centuries, going back to the monasteries of medieval times, or even farther, in the Christian tradition, to those early abbas and ammas of the desert tradition. A deeper look at this uniquely Christ-centered spiritual direction makes clear that this spiritual practice is not about getting the world to move in your direction; rather, it is about you moving in God's direction—a far more humble proposition.

In fact, to speak of Christ-centered spiritual direction is to speak of spiritual *and vocational* direction. The spiritual and vocational dimensions of a person's life simply cannot be separated. Why? Because by its very nature a robust experience of Christ-centered spiritual direction takes you directly into the heart of the mystery of life in Christ—specifically, the paschal mystery. This work of dying and rising to new life unfolds over the course of a lifetime, touching and shaping and defining every dimension of human life and the life of all of creation.

This mystery of the dying and the rising to new life which lies at the heart of all living things shapes the core of every Christian sacrament and the whole of sacramental life. This rhythm of dying and receiving new life indeed is a universal—or "catholic"—experience, raised to a redemptive level in the life of the church. In Christ-centered direction the very rhythm of the dying and rising which defines the Christ event forms the core understanding of what God is up to in the directee's life.

While I am Catholic, I do not expect you to be. Several of my directees are clergy and lay men and women of the various Christian denominations. What we cherish, wrestle with, and share in common is the inescapable engagement in the paschal mystery, the dying and the rising to new life.

Even if you are Catholic, I do not expect that your expressions of faith will be just like mine, because your life's narrative is unique to you and prismed through the facets of your unique personality. Your life will be graced and burnished in ways that will call forth your particular and eternal dignity and beauty, and I will be graced and burnished in ways unique to me.

But I do expect one thing: that in your life you already will have experienced the dying and the rising in more ways than you may have imagined. Even your living of your vows and sacred commitments—whether expressed publicly or honored interiorly—will expose you and render you vulnerable to the ineffable mystery of God's movement in your life.

What, then, *is* Christ-centered spiritual and vocational direction? How shall we describe it? I propose that it is a *relationship* of a trained and appropriately gifted director with the directee in the work of God-centered listening: in Scripture, in conversation, in exploring life experience in light of the church's liturgical and sacramental practice and body of wisdom; and listening, too, in the silent spaces between the spoken words. In the course of conversation, and in a very fine-tuned way, the director listens with the outer ear to the directee, and with the inner ear to the Holy Spirit.

Spiritual direction indeed is "holy conversation." Yet the term "holy conversation" can sound too superficial for the deep, interior, and sacred work of the dynamic process that lies at the heart of this graced relationship. Spiritual directors and authors Francis Kelly Nemeck and Marie Theresa Coombs describe spiritual direction as the work of guiding others through their "passover in the Lord, … a unique participation in another's spiritual regeneration, deification, transformation."[2] Spiritual direction is no small work. In its richest expressions spiritual direction is an individual's real spiritual birthing into the fullness of life in Christ, through the wise and graced counsel of another.

In the chapters ahead we will explore in detail, first, what constitutes an authentically Christ-centered spiritual direction relationship. And second, we will explore the dynamics of the spiritual and vocational direction process and the topics and life circumstances deserving of this holy conversation.

Christ-centered spiritual direction integrates reflection on the directee's circumstances with the wisdom of Scripture and the church's rich liturgical and sacramental life and body of teaching. Why do we include these elements? Because these elements of the actual lived Tradition of the church exist in service to the core expression of Christian faith in the human experience of the paschal mystery. This integration of personal experience and the church's rich heritage, properly called theological reflection, is sadly missing in much of adult faith development, yet this integration is vital to spiritual growth and one's maturing into the fullness of authentic personhood.

The unique approach I bring to spiritual and vocational direction, and

---

[2] Francis Kelly Nemeck, OMI, and Marie Theresa Coombs, *The Way of Spiritual Direction* (Collegeville, MN: Michael Glazer/The Liturgical Press, 1985), 16.

which I have found unusually fruitful, unites my areas of inquiry and interest: what I call "classic Christ-centered spiritual direction" shaped by the paschal mystery, as noted above, united with charism discernment, and discernment of how God is calling the directee to fullness of personhood through life circumstances, vocational lifestyle, unique gifts, and personal mission. I believe deeply that *every* baptized man and woman is anointed to live, as Jesus lived, generously and lovingly for the sake of the world. I count it a distinct blessing when I can assist a directee in the fine-tuned work of preparing the soul for such engagement in life.

Moving in God's Direction is not a "how to" book for would-be spiritual directors. If you seek to become a spiritual director, you will need to work in a committed way within the scope of a rigorous curriculum, under the guidance of an experienced spiritual director who also is qualified to teach the art, science, and theological foundation of spiritual direction. Such a program will equip you for the deep work of personal discernment and formation for this ministry.

Moving in God's Direction is designed, however, to serve two audiences. First, the book serves spiritual directors who seek a means to integrate their living faith experience, and a deepened understanding of the dynamics of God's calling and individuals' free and loving response, with their presence to others in this specialized form of "holy conversation." Second, the book is designed to be used by individuals—including directees—who are searching for a deeper understanding of what to expect, not only in truly Christ-centered spiritual and vocational direction but in the lifelong endeavor of becoming their authentic self-in-God.

This book is meant to be used. Take notes, capture ideas, highlight passages that resonate with you or challenge you or expand your horizons. Each chapter ends with reflection questions designed to help you to apply the chapter's material to your own experience. These questions also can serve to spark small group discussion.

If you are alive, you are moving. And if you are moving, you are moving in some direction. What does it mean to move in God's direction? It means to move both *in* the direction and *at* the direction of the Holy Spirit. As Jesus says in his holy conversation with Nicodemus, the wind "blows where it wills, … so it is with everyone who is born of the Spirit" (John 3:8).

Here is an overview of what we will cover:

In Part I, "Getting the Conversation Going: The Spirit Meets the Need," we will examine what goes into the formation of the Christ-centered spiritual director who seeks to be well-equipped to meet the spiritual and vocational needs of baptized men and women living in our twenty-first century church and world.

In Part II, "The Maturing Conversation: The Spiritual Meets the Vocational," we will look at topics of life experience and spiritual growth that are appropriate to Christ-centered spiritual and vocational direction. These areas of inquiry uniquely guide a person toward vocational fullness of personhood according to their anointing in Baptism and Confirmation. We will conclude with a focus on how spiritual and vocational direction supports the man or woman of mature faith in the work of standing in the place of Jesus in our twenty-first century world.

As you can see, *Moving in God's Direction* covers a lot of territory. We will take it one thoughtful step at a time. I am glad that you can join me in exploring this amazing lifelong journey of "moving in God's direction."

PART I

GETTING THE CONVERSATION GOING

The Spirit Meets the Need

In Part I we will explore how moving in God's direction is essential to growth toward fullness of personhood in Christ—not merely for the sake of personal holiness but for the sake of this world which God still so loves. We will look at what goes into the formation of the Christ-centered spiritual and vocational director and the direction relationship, and why it all matters.

1

MOVING IN GOD'S DIRECTION

The Spiritual and the Vocational are One

At the Coffee People kiosk in the Portland International Airport I saw a sign by the tip jar: "If you fear change, leave it here." I smiled. The writer in me appreciated the play on words. But deep down I intuited what many people feel but seldom talk about when the prospect of change irrupts in their life. And along with unsought change in one's circumstances—even if it is change for the better, or even long-desired change—often comes the unnerving feeling of being stalked by a dark cold presence of fear.

From the very point of inception, every living being is launched on a trajectory of life where a process of continual evolvement is the norm. So why do we fear change when in reality we are "hard wired" for it as a constant in the continuum of life? Why might *you* fear change? In the best scenarios, change comes as a desired and favorable shift in circumstances. Or change may come as unexpected relief. Change can nudge you forward along your desired path. But change also can hurl you into a place of existential uncertainty.

Change is a "frontier" experience, moving you at least interiorly, if not physically, to the threshold—or even across the threshold—of the unknown.

Motivated by hope, or sometimes by sheer desperation, you may *choose* to initiate change in your life. You may choose to marry this particular person, or find a new job, or sell the house, or pursue studies for the next phase in your career.[3] But deep down you know that in order to achieve this change in your circumstances you are stepping into a zone of uncertainty, moving intentionally toward an unexplored personal horizon.

The spouse of your choosing may not be the right spouse. The job you seek, for all its perks and better pay, may leave you longing for the work for which you were better gifted. When you commit yourself to one option over all others, you submit yourself to what *you* have chosen, and you have no way of actually knowing what this choice, this change, and this commitment will demand of you. Yet committing yourself wholeheartedly to this particular option, even if it turns out to be the wrong one, puts your life into play in a way that "keeping your options open" never can. Life offers no guarantees that you will make the right choices all the time. When you initiate change in your life, you submit your autonomy to forces far greater than yourself.

Spiritual Movement

Already our language and understanding of change becomes complex. Every day we do initiate change in our lives. We shop for what's new, we purchase the latest technologies, we consume. We do things we have never done before because we can. We set in motion what we want in life.

But the honest spiritual truth is that none of us is the center of our universe. Indeed, when we initiate real change, substantial change, in our lives we do submit our autonomy to forces greater than ourselves. For the Christian man or woman, that greater force is the unseen Spirit of the living Christ. For

---

[3] I recall, at age 29, seemingly out of the blue, I entered graduate school. I intentionally took all the steps to apply for admission and to enroll. Still, I felt gripped with fear, sitting in the school dining hall, alone, and at the table in the furthest corner, as I created my class schedule. Intentional change, yes, but the reality of it, and the overwhelming sense that I was working with larger forces in shaping my future, unnerved me.

the baptized man or woman, we call this experience of wished-for—or sometimes courageous—change "moving into the mystery of God."

Who you *are*—that self at the core of your being—is the *spiritual* dimension of your personhood; who you are *becoming* in response to God's continuous invitation is the *vocational* dimension of your life. God *is* "Frontier," the great I AM who urges us forward beyond the safe parameters of our known world. Often we find ourselves impelled by a desiring greater than our own, and find ourselves awakening to God's desiring in us.

This emotional, spiritual, relational, or professional growth, when it is of God's desiring, occurs seamlessly, we might say, within the fabric of our life. We are full-fledged participants in this enterprise called "life," and our lives are imbued with the divine integrity of the Incarnation. At every growth point we seem to be offered two options: We can grow according to God's movement already in motion in our life, or we can resist. Over time you discover, perhaps to your astonishment, that God takes *your* life seriously.

Moving in God's direction is real spiritual work, and requires actual movement—yours, certainly. But more important, moving in God's direction is about you giving the Holy Spirit the freedom to move in you and through the circumstances of your life in God's great work of bringing you to fullness of personhood. The real spiritual work is not in *choosing* (as though you were the initiator), but in *discerning,* detecting, getting a sense of God's movement already at work in your life.

This divine-human movement concerns your growth and your coming to fullness of personhood. Even more, this divine-human movement is about your participation in God's plan for this world which you touch, this world which God still so loves. In time you discover that moving in God's direction is not only your spiritual work but indeed the spiritual work of all of humankind and all of creation. Ultimately, this movement in God's direction is the all-encompassing work of the risen Lord himself, from whose resurrection radiates the magnetic power to "draw all things to himself."[4] The New Testament canticles resonate with this movement, this spiritual awakening of all of humankind and all of creation to the inescapable divine call to fullness of being-in-God.[5]

Vocational Movement

As a baptized man or woman, God's direction of your journey through life is a given, whether you are conscious of it or not. While you may not be fully aware of God's movement, your intent to be open to God's movement is often invitation enough for the Holy Spirit to get to work.[6] Being open to moving in God's direction of your life requires an ever awakening partnership, your increasingly wholehearted participation in a living relationship with the living God. Indeed, the dignity of being human, the dignity of the personhood of each individual, generates from this extraordinary divine-human partnership.

In the best of all circumstances you journey through your life *at* God's direction. But more important is journeying through life *in* God's direction. Journeying *at* God's direction and *in* God's direction are the key vocational elements of your life. Both modes of journeying—*at* God's direction and *in* God's direction—are guided by the Holy Spirit to whom you give your explicit or at least subconscious *Yes.* When you are vocationally alive, the dynamic and magnetic pull of life-in-God becomes, ultimately, irresistible.

---

[4] See John 12:32: "And when I am lifted up from the earth, I will draw everyone to myself."

[5] See Colossians 1:12–20, esp. v. 17: "[the Beloved Son] is before all things, / and in him all things hold together." See also Ephesians 1:3–10, esp. v. 10: "… as a plan for the fullness of times, to sum up all things in Christ, in heaven and on earth"; and Philippians 2:6–11, esp. v. 10: "… at the name of Jesus / every knee should bend, / of those in heaven and on earth and under the earth."

[6] I think here of the oft-quoted prayer of Thomas Merton: "My Lord God, I have no idea where I am going … and the fact that I think I am following your will does not mean that I am actually doing so. But I believe that the desire to please you does in fact please you." See Thomas Merton, *Thoughts in Solitude,* in Lawrence S. Cunningham, ed., *Thomas Merton: Spiritual Master* (New York: Paulist, 1992), 243.

As your baptism into the living Christ unfolds over the course of your life, you undergo a spiritual awakening. Your anointing works its intended effect, and you begin to discover, in the particular circumstances of your life, that you really are *from* God, that your life is now lived *for* God, and that you are *returning to* God.[7] This ongoing spiritual awakening serves to expand your capacity to take seriously your life and your purpose in this world. And this successively deeper awakening leads you, over time, to discover the trajectory of your life as the trajectory of one of God's anointed: You have been sent, and you are returning.

Such discovery of being-in-God and of one's mission in life is the desired and optimal outcome of a life of faith that often is fraught with change and unpredicted detours. Yet the Christian claim that all things hold together in Christ still applies, as twentieth-century French Jesuit theologian Pierre Teilhard de Chardin eloquently expressed: "Christ, his heart a fire, capable of penetrating everywhere and, gradually, spreading everywhere."[8]

Discerning God's movement as a uniquely vocational work in one's life brings consolation, peace, and a sense of inclusion and meaning to those who would have "eyes to see" the finely calibrated movement of the Holy Spirit in the circumstances of their lives.[9] Out of many possible options, you may find yourself repeatedly drawn to one particular option. You may experience a breaking away from your familiar path to pursue what is both new and yet integrative with who you have been becoming all along.

When directees are vocationally moving in God's direction they will experience the encouragement and affirmation of others, especially of those

---

[7] This notion of being from God, for God, and returning to God runs throughout the vocational writings of Nemeck and Coombs. See their *Called by God: A Theology of Vocation and Lifelong Commitment* (Eugene, OR: Wipf and Stock, 2001) and *Discerning Vocations to Marriage, Celibacy and Singlehood* (Eugene, OR: Wipf and Stock, 2001) (hereafter *Discerning Vocations*).

[8] Pierre Teilhard de Chardin, SJ, *The Heart of the Matter* (trans. René Hague) (San Diego: Harcourt, 1978), 58.

[9] See Nemeck and Coombs, *The Way of Spiritual Direction,* 114–118.

within the Christian community, because others will perceive them as alive, vibrant, effective, and really "coming into their own." They will experience a deep-seated and abiding peace, even in the midst of uncertainty or unusual challenge. Through no determined effort on their part, their lives will manifest fruits of the Holy Spirit—love, joy, peace, patience, kindness, goodness, fidelity, gentleness, and self-control.[10]

Additional signs that affirm directees in discerning the ways of God's calling—vocational discernment—include their willingness to actually live and move intentionally in God's direction in authentic and courageous ways according to their gifting, and to freely move *by faith*. This means actually stepping out rather than waiting for clear signs that one is making the right move that will ensure the greatest likelihood of success at the lowest risk.

Moving *at* God's direction and moving *in* God's direction is the radically self-involving and holy work that lies at the heart of spiritual and vocational direction. Spiritual direction is not first of all about "solving problems," although real and immediate concerns in your life may be the material you bring to a session. And spiritual direction is not primarily about "getting advice," although you may come away from a session with fresh insight into a circumstance or challenge or stuck point in your life. Your pursuit of spiritual and vocational direction is a bold and generous expression of your Yes to the life—*your* life—which God already has set in motion.

Spiritual and vocational direction is about discovering how *God* is moving in your life, especially in the difficult or confusing situations, the tragic situations, the lost opportunities, the unbidden invitations, the restlessness with feeling stuck, the unexpected openings. And spiritual and vocational direction is

---

[10] See Galatians 5:22–23. These truly are fruits of the Holy Spirit and not the fruits of any determined personal effort to be loving, joyful, patient, gentle, and so on, any more than an apple is the fruit of a tree that set out for itself the goal of producing such round, juicy, rose-cheeked edible delights. Yet Jesus assures us that by these fruits which manifest in our lives we will be known (see Matthew 7:17–20).

about discerning how you are responding as you move through these unique circumstances, at this time in your life, in God's direction—moving more deeply into the mystery of God.

Bringing It Home

1. What has been one situation in my life when I felt forced to change, and where perhaps I pushed back or resisted or hid as long as I could? How has that situation become resolved? What unexpected grace or good has come of it?

2. Considering where I am in my life now, compared to five years ago, what evidence do I find that I am actually moving in God's direction? Compared to two years ago, what evidence do I find? Compared to six months ago?

3. What gives me hope about my life right now?

Hold this Thought

I invite the Holy Spirit to be fruitful *in* my life
and *through* my life.

2

WHAT TO LOOK FOR IN A

CHRIST-CENTERED SPIRITUAL DIRECTOR

Seven Core Elements

I have never believed in the myth that "one size fits all." Just a quick glance at the people around me affirms what a silly notion this is. One day a friend quite flatly expressed the truth of the matter in four words: "One size fits some."

Indeed. And it is the same with spiritual directors—even with that particular segment which we are considering, Christ-centered spiritual and vocational directors. We each are as unique as the gifts we have been given, the skills and talents we have developed, and the challenges and unbidden graces we have encountered. We each are as particular as the experiences we have undergone and the personalities that make us each so uniquely lovable.

Still, no matter the particular capacities and personality profile, some foundational pieces do need to be well established and consistently in place in the life and practice of a spiritual and vocational director—just as you would rightly expect of your physician or your accountant or your pastor. Perhaps as much unknowingly as intentionally, Christ-centered spiritual directors work with the Holy Spirit, but this does not mean that they "wing it."

What makes for a good Christ-centered spiritual and vocational director? Based on my experience as both director and directee, I propose seven core elements.

1. The Call

The first core element that needs to be present within a Christ-centered spiritual director is *a clear sense of calling.* Not just an intuitive hunch, not just a feeling that you would be good at spiritual direction because you are good at listening, or because you like to help people who are in tough situations or undergoing emotional or spiritual anguish.

A clear sense of calling emerges over time, and oftentimes in very clear ways at very specific moments. Overall, you may notice a consistent pattern of being unusually effective in listening to others without feeling distracted or drained in the process. You may notice a pattern of people actually seeking you out—seeking *you* rather than the person next to you, or another equally trained spiritual director—because somehow they intuit that *you* possess the capacity to listen and really hear what they are trying to say. In fact, people may tell you, "When I talk to you I feel really listened to; for the first time I feel heard." These words are always a grace, and an indicator of the direction in which the Holy Spirit may be leading you.

You may notice, over time, an unusual ability to quickly see the big picture of a person's situation, name it, and cut straight to the heart of the matter. You may notice a pattern, over time, of people coming away from a conversation with you saying, "You have such an ability to name what's going on; you really help me to see my life from a new perspective." Or you may notice that people who live at the margins of society or at the margins of social acceptability seek you out just to talk, sensing that *you* will understand them and not turn them away. They may express their gratitude that in your presence they felt welcomed as a real person.

So a clear sense of calling comes, over time, as you reflect on your experience and on consistent patterns of experience with others. You may notice especially the situations in which you seem most effective without undue strain. But there is another equally important experience of calling to this work of love which we call spiritual and vocational direction. It is the experience of actually being *called forth by others*—within the Christian community or even by strangers whom you may meet incidentally who have a clear-eyed capacity to accurately name your giftedness.

Many years back I remember my friend Mary calling to me across the church parking lot. Mary was full of enthusiasm for the spiritual direction formation course she was taking, and was quite clear—insistent, even—that I needed to be in the class, too. She approached me with the zeal of a recruiter on commission. "You'd be a great spiritual director," Mary insisted. "No, I don't think that's for me," I said, firmly pushing back. And the more Mary insisted, the more I resisted. Why? For one simple and selfish reason: To be a spiritual director, I would need to *receive* spiritual direction myself. And self-sufficient introvert that I was, I clearly was not going to "process my stuff" with anyone else.

I thought I was off the hook until Mary showed up at my door early one Wednesday morning, seat-belted me into her car, and drove me two hours up Interstate 5 to the class. End of debate—although, thankfully, not the end of the friendship. When I walked into the classroom the teacher looked at me with a knowing twinkle in her eye and said, "I've heard all about you." I took my seat, gave myself to the process, and never looked back.

Being called forth by the Christian community as one who is appropriately gifted is an important dimension of this vocational "calling." It is not merely a matter of people recognizing your gifts and talents and skills, and urging, "You would be great at this." What's really at work is the Holy Spirit, stirring in the hearts and minds and imagination of others, calling you, urging you, nudging you to move in God's direction in this particular way.

2. Particular Abilities and Gifts

The second core element that makes for a good spiritual director is the particular cluster of *innate abilities* and *spiritual gifts*—or *charisms*—that gives evidence of real anointing for this deep work of holy conversation with another.

Innate Abilities in the Director

Of the innate abilities, I look for a capacity in the spiritual director to *listen deeply,* reverently, and with a confidential heart. This does not mean listening for every detail of what the directee says, or even catching the narrative in its entirety. Rather, what matters is listening for what the Holy Spirit wants the director to hear—which might be one small phrase spoken once, early on, in a directee's extended presentation of a complex situation. The director listens reverently, knowing that what tumbles forth from the heart and mind and understanding of the directee is the raw wet clay which God is still shaping into something worthy and new.

Coupled with listening is *patience*. A highly desirable ability of good spiritual directors is their capacity to instinctively set aside their own busyness to be fully present to the other. Or, if the moment is not right, they are able to graciously say so, so as to not diminish the dignity of the other, and schedule a more appropriate time when the director can engage in undistracted listening. If you are by temperament more given to putting out fires on the spot, you may discern that you are better suited to a crisis hotline, or frontline social work, or some similar "emotional first responder" line of work. Spiritual direction is most effective not in the heat of the moment but in an environment conducive to reflection on circumstances, contemplative holy silences, and undistracted attentiveness to the subtle movements of the Holy Spirit.

Kindness is another innate quality of a good spiritual director. What is it about kindness that makes it so desirable in a director? Kindness communicates a core reality: We are *of a kind*. Kindness in a spiritual director affirms that *the language of the human heart is spoken here*. The opening pages of Scripture tell us that kindness has a theological foundation: We are all *of a kind* because we are all made in the image and likeness of God, as Genesis 1 so beautifully describes. The person of kindness communicates: *We are in this business of life together*—a phrase we can confidently speak because God has spoken it first.

That said, overt empathy, or the expression of feeling the other's pain, is *not* a helpful quality in the spiritual director. The phrase to remember here is simple: "It's all about you; it's not about me." To say to a troubled directee, "I know exactly what you're going through," or even to say, "I understand," frustrates the possibility of the directee going deeper into difficult material. In my own practice, on two occasions directees have described deeply painful experiences that expressed word for word some deeply painful experiences of my own in earlier years. In the moment of listening I simply made mental note of the material which the directee had unknowingly called up within me, and revisited it later when I could be open to what the Holy Spirit wanted to reveal to me in this incident. My work in the direction session, however, was to be fully present to the directee and to the ways the Holy Spirit was at work in this individual in this particular situation.

Empathic phrases such as, "Oh, how wonderful" or "You must feel relieved," or "How sad" do not work in spiritual direction for another reason, too. They can subconsciously condition the directee to report in future sessions those things that likely will elicit from the director the emotional support, or praise, or even judgment, that the directee may unknowingly seek to stay spiritually in a safe or even a stuck place. The director who is empathic by nature must be aware of the potentially limiting effects of empathy expressed in the direction session.

In addition to skills and innate abilities, some charisms, too, are identified as particularly desirable in a spiritual director. Charisms, or gifts of the Holy Spirit which are given to each baptized person expressly for the good of others, cannot be acquired through prayer or practice.[11] The charisms classically identified as highly desirable for Christ-centered spiritual direction include the following:

Encouragement, the charism by which the director interiorly senses *who* God desires the directee to be and detects ways in which the directee may be spiritually unfree. The person with this charism of Encouragement has an unusual ability to see when another person is not at ease to be himself or herself. In the presence of this charism the other experiences a freedom to be authentic, to feel acknowledged and heard and understood, and to encounter unexpected hope. When the charism of Encouragement is present in the director, then through the director's presence, listening, and words the directee becomes interiorly free to enter into the place of fear, brokenness, uncertainty, or pain in order to say what needs to be said and to experience renewed strength of heart.

Evangelism, the charism by which the director quickly perceives how the directee needs to experience a rekindling of relationship with God, with Jesus, or with the Christian community, or how the directee needs to take that relationship to a deeper, more responsible and mature level. This charism expresses a distinct challenge and irresistible invitation to a living relationship with the risen Christ. When the charism of Evangelism is present in the director,

[11] See "What's in Your Spiritual Toolkit" in chapter 8 for further discussion of charisms. While the Catholic Church does not set the charisms at any fixed number, typically spiritual gifts inventories include twenty or so. The "Called and Gifted" workshop of the Catherine of Siena Institute (www.siena.org) addresses twenty-four readily identifiable charisms, ranging from the more common (such as charisms of Service, Administration, Mercy, and Hospitality) to the less common or even quite rare (such as charisms of Intercessory Prayer, Healing, Prophecy, and Discernment of Spirits). The charisms you receive in "seed" form in Baptism and which mature as you mature in your role in the reign of God are your charisms for life. As you mature in your use of the charisms they begin to "describe" you, your work, and your fruitfulness. You cannot acquire additional charisms through practice or training or prayer. Your charisms guide the trajectory of your life and the fulfillment of your purpose in life and therefore have an important vocational dimension.

the directee may feel an opening of heart toward Jesus' offer of unconditional love and mature friendship, or experience the urge toward conversion of heart and a burning desire to serve the reign of God more wholeheartedly.

Wisdom, the charism by which the director quickly and accurately sees the larger picture of the directee's situation, and is able to accurately diagnose what needs to be addressed and what practical steps need to be taken. Directors with the charism of Wisdom are known for the piercing clarity of their insight and their unusual ability to frame a situation within its fuller context. When the charism of Wisdom is present in the director, the directee will sense a "right diagnosis," and will be able now to get quickly to the heart of the matter.

Many of the charisms—such as Hospitality, Mercy, Helps, Prophecy, and Discernment of Spirits—can be at the service of the spiritual and vocational direction relationship. However, Encouragement, Evangelism, and Wisdom are unusually beneficial and much sought in traditional spiritual and vocational direction. When the charisms are present in the director, the director will be unable to *not* use them in service of the directee.

Because the charisms are actual expressions of the Holy Spirit they cannot be effectively suppressed, except in the presence of grave moral obstacles, in which case the director likely would be unable to engage effectively in the quality and depth of authentic conversation required in spiritual direction. And if these charisms most helpful to spiritual direction are not already given by the Holy Spirit, the director cannot do anything to "develop" them. Discernment of the presence of charisms most helpful to spiritual direction is crucial to discerning whether one is called by God to be a spiritual director. Evidence of other clusters of charisms at work within the director may indicate that God may have in mind some other work or ministry.

3. Formation

A third and obvious core element for a spiritual director is *formation*, including training, practicum, and critical feedback. Many certification programs exist for formation of spiritual directors, and each program has its particular focus and appeal. Online research can help a potential director to determine which program, which formation process, and which particular spiritual focus will provide the best fit and be most beneficial. It is not unusual that the training can be so intense, and the future director's desire to "get it right" can be so strong, that the practicum experience can feel artificial or forced or just plain stiff as cardboard. That is because emerging spiritual directors usually need time to grow into their role, to "find their voice," and to feel established in the flow and grace of their particular style of spiritual direction. Hence, an extended practicum, or ongoing supervision, can give helpful guidance once the director and the Holy Spirit gain momentum in this ministry.

The course work and training in spiritual direction hopefully will be theologically relevant, psychologically sound, integrative of the many dimensions of human experience, and spiritually meaningful. In the course of time many directors discover that training in spiritual direction alone is not enough. A director may begin to sense a particular ability to work with, say, people in prison, people with profound disabilities, or people recuperating from the trauma of abuse or violence. A director may discern an unusual ability to work with people who are socially marginalized, people with terminal illness, or any other distinctive population. Here the director may seek out resources, or even an advanced degree, to gain a fuller understanding of the spiritual challenges and opportunities which this particular population of directees will encounter.

Critical feedback in a practicum setting is important to a spiritual director, too. Not designed to be "picky" or "criticizing" in its content, critical feedback can provide honest encouragement and gently delivered reflection on how the director is doing in a direction session and in the director-directee relationship overall. Learning to listen to the Holy Spirit while listening to the directee can at first feel like multitasking. If the gifting is there, then in time and with practice you will get it. You will not get lost in the details and your words will begin to flow with a hidden grace.

4. Ongoing Discernment

The fourth core element, which flows in part from the director's training and gifting and in part from the director's personal experience as a director, is *a deeper discernment of calling.* As you mature in your spiritual direction practice the vocational question is not so much: *Is God calling me to this work?* You will know, before long, whether the answer is Yes or No.

Rather, the intriguing question is: *In what deeper ways* is God calling me to this work? In what particular ways, in this place, with these people, at this time in my life? Which particular people, or types of people, or types of concerns seem either to attract me or to actually seek me out? What interests are emerging in my own life? What do I feel drawn to study in order to partner more closely with the Holy Spirit in the healing and animating work of spiritual direction? Over time the richly experienced spiritual director will discover a tapestry-like practice which intricately weaves together the various threads of inquiry, study, prayer, and integrative reflection.

The tapestry of my own spiritual and vocational direction practice reveals various threads including graduate studies in theology with a particular focus in liturgical spirituality. These studies, combined with an ongoing reflection on the rhythms of dying and receiving new life in my personal experience, have given me a context of faith for my own journey and a sensitivity to the paschal mystery at work in directees' lives. My practice also incorporates an awareness of charisms at work in directees' lives, thanks to the ongoing study of charisms and my years of practice in discerning charisms as indicators of God's calling. Reflecting on these various threads at work in my spiritual and vocational direction practice reveals the deeper ways the Holy Spirit is calling upon me to be the ears and heart and presence of the risen Lord to these people whom the Spirit has entrusted to my care.

Spiritual direction is something like writing: Each needs content in order to express or reveal something. For the spiritual director this content is the unique cluster of elements that make up not just human living but the director's particular experience of human living, including inquiry and the nature of that inquiry, study and the focus of that study, prayer and the content of prayer, relationships and the quality of those relationships, givenness to particular causes or social concerns and the particular passion for the Gospel which the director reveals. Through actual engagement in these elements of human experience the director's life will begin to model the mature Christ-centered life.

5. Ongoing Growth

The fifth core element in the Christ-centered spiritual director's practice is *ongoing personal, spiritual, and theological growth.* Personal growth might be something as simple as starting a new hobby, pursuing a healthier lifestyle, planting a garden, learning a new kind of cooking, taking up a new outdoor activity. For me recently, personal growth took a leap forward when I bought my first camera, affording me a whole new level of discovery and engagement with the overlooked wonders of nearby nature. The point of personal growth is to intentionally expand outward the boundaries of your experience. Taking on the challenge of learning something new, or engaging in new skills or activities, moves your personal world deeper into the circle of human experience.

As with personal growth, spiritual growth is intentional. Opportunities for spiritual growth continually present themselves. Loss of health or the unexpected return of health, loss of a loved one or the forging of a new relationship, loss of a cherished dream or the opening of unexpected opportunity —all the ebb and flow of life—are invitations to enter more deeply into the paschal mystery which is central to Christian faith. Spiritual growth is essential to achieving fullness of your unique expression of personhood. For spiritual and vocational directors, spiritual growth is not only important for the lifelong personal journey into God. It is a vital dimension of what the director models to directees.

Theological growth may include pursuit of a personal course of study or an academic path toward a degree or certification. But at the very least theological growth comes through the discipline of theological reflection—bringing your experience into dynamic conversation with Scripture and the wisdom of church teaching.[12] The matters which you bring to theological reflection can range from persistent petty habits which block authentic relationship, to unexpected opportunity, to unresolved grave moral failings. Theological reflection can generate a dynamic tension between your present circumstances and an interior urge toward holiness—a dynamic tension that seeks resolution in action, or in conversion of heart, mind, attitude, and spirit. Theological reflection on the circumstances of your life can also open the door to the sweet grace of forgiveness, unexpected affirmation and blessing, and the assurance that you are on the path of authentic life, the life that bears your name and no one else's.

6. Commitment to Prayer

The sixth core element in the formation of a Christ-centered spiritual director is *a deep and abiding commitment to prayer.* In my initial interview with potential directees, if they do not ask me to describe my prayer life, I tell them how I pray—not to win their favor but to reveal to them something of the soil in which my roots are planted. In no way do I expect my directees to have a prayer life just like mine. But they need to feel confident that where my heart lies is where they will find treasures of encouragement and spiritual sustenance for their own lives. Prayer—and a steadfast prayer life—matters tremendously for those engaged in the intentional work of moving others in God's direction.

The two types of prayer which shape my life are solitary prayer and liturgical prayer. And for me, given my solitary lifestyle, there is a place where the two overlap.

---

[12] For a good study on the art and science of theological reflection, with process for application, see Patricia O'Connell Killen and John de Beer, *The Art of Theological Reflection* (New York: Crossroad, 1994, 2002). The topic will be addressed in greater depth in chapter 11.

Solitary prayer is, in essence, an encounter of the self before God, or more accurately, the self *in* God. For me, this solitary prayer is shaped by the wisdom in St. Paul's letter to the Romans: "for we do not know how to pray as we ought, but the Spirit itself intercedes with inexpressible groanings" (Romans 8:26). Solitary prayer is the soul's experience of remaining in God, an interior and abiding communion in God. Solitary prayer is the soul already feasting at the banquet of the Holy Trinity.[13]

I distinguish solitary prayer from devotional prayer. Devotional prayer can include formula petitionary prayers and novenas, which can carry an overlay of worry. In solitary prayer, by contrast, the soul becomes incapable of worry about the subject of one's prayer. Solitary prayer does not really ask for anything, but rather, recognizes that what is truly needed is already assured. It is prayer which invites the soul simply to abide in God.

In contrast to solitary prayer, liturgical prayer is prayer of the church. The structure of liturgical prayer is quite simple: It encompasses the dying and the rising, the paschal mystery, of Christ Jesus, and the dying and the rising in him within the human experience. The Liturgy of the Word, the Liturgy of the Eucharist, and the Liturgy of the Hours[14] all carry this foundational movement: from life, through dying to self, to receiving new life in the risen Lord.

In a very real sense "liturgy" and "life in Christ" are the same thing. St. Paul writes, "For you have died, and your life is hidden with Christ in

---

[13] For a further development of this notion of indwelling, see my essay "Meditation on Three Words" in *Touching the Reign of God: Bringing Theological Reflection to Daily Life* (Eugene, OR: Wipf and Stock, 2009), 50–56. Jesus speaks to the Twelve of this "remaining in" God and "remaining in" him; see John 15:4–10.

[14] Evolving from the Jewish practice of gathering for common public praying of the psalms at set hours throughout the day, the early church similarly gathered, understanding the psalms to prefigure the praise and intercession of the risen Lord Jesus. Today the Liturgy of the Hours, or Divine Office, is the church's principal prayer of praise and petition. "In fact," we read in the General Instruction of the Liturgy of the Hours, "it is the prayer of the Church with Christ and to Christ." See "General Instruction of the Liturgy of the Hours" (abridged) in *Christian Prayer: The Liturgy of the Hours* (New York: Catholic Book Publishing, 1976), 8–19.

2 | WHAT TO LOOK FOR

God" (Colossians 3:3). And again he writes, "I live, no longer I, but Christ lives in me" (Galatians 2:20). In each of these expressions of the paschal mystery we encounter God at work in our lives. Not surprisingly, liturgical prayer is spiritually dangerous prayer, by which the individual and the Christian community as a whole undergo a dying to self in order to receive new life in Christ. Liturgy, then, is our ritual way of learning how to die to self and enter, through Jesus the crucified and risen Christ, into the mystery of God.[15] I believe it is imperative for the Christ-centered spiritual and vocational director to actively engage in liturgical prayer in order to recognize and cooperate with the deeper work of the Holy Spirit in the spiritual direction session.

I pray the Liturgy of the Hours not in community but alone, so that for me it is both liturgical prayer and prayer offered in solitude.[16] Yet even here I pray not alone but as the voice of Jesus and in communion with the entire church—past, present, and future—because, as St. Paul affirms, all ages belong to Christ, and Christ belongs to God.[17] The beauty of praying the psalms of Morning and Evening and Night prayer alone, I have found, is that the soul becomes free to linger over and enter more deeply into one phrase or another, one stanza or another, and to be richly fed on these treasures. The slow "breathing" of each line, in the rhythm of the natural intake and outflow of breath, allows lines of the psalms to become embedded in the soul and also in the flesh, the bone, down to the marrow of the bone.[18]

I frequently encourage lay men and women to pray the Liturgy of the

---

[15] See Robert Taft, SJ, *Liturgy of the Hours in East and West: The Origins of the Divine Office and Its Meaning for Today* (2nd revised ed.) (Collegeville, MN: Liturgical Press, 1986, 1993). Ideas presented here are taken from my unpublished notes from Taft's lecture at Mount Angel Abbey, St. Benedict, OR, on October 26, 1999. Ideas expressed here also come from my unpublished notes from lectures in "Liturgy in a Formative Environment," (www.ilmdayton.org/life.htm), a two-week immersion in the liturgical life of the church, taught by Joyce Ann Zimmerman, CPPS, and Kathleen Harmon, SND de N.

[16] See my essay "Let My Prayer Arise" in *Touching the Reign of God*, 72–87.

[17] See 1 Corinthians 3:22–23.

[18] For a description of this internalizing of lines of the psalms, see my essay, "These Bones," in *Touching the Reign of God*, 57–59.

Hours, alone or in community, and I am amazed at how many already do. The hidden beauty of the Liturgy of the Hours is that it literally interrupts your day in order to draw you consciously back to center, to the spiritual and mindful place of dying and rising, becoming as close to you as the systolic-diastolic rhythm of your beating heart.

The spiritual and vocational director who consciously and wholeheartedly practices both prayer of solitude and liturgical prayer eventually awakens to the deeper understanding of *why* we pray: We are impelled to pray because *Jesus is not yet finished praying to his Father.* Over time, and in this deeper understanding of prayer, one comes to share in the one heartbeat of God, and to pray with the breath of the risen Christ, the breath which is the Holy Spirit. This deep interior formation is an unspoken but immeasurable gift which the director—knowingly or unknowingly—offers to the directee.

7. Willingness to Receive Direction

Finally, the seventh core element in the ongoing formation of the Christ-centered spiritual director is *a willingness to receive spiritual direction.* For some directors, this can be the humbling piece. For others, sharing details of their spiritual journey with another trusted director or person of wise counsel can come as a relief. Still for others, slowing down to intentionally, prayerfully, and lovingly reflect on and give words to God's movement in their own life can feel like an interruption. Even Jesus had to urge the Twelve to "come away to a quiet place to rest."[19] Jesus also urged his followers, "Come to me, all you who labor and are burdened, and I will give you rest. ... I am meek and humble of heart; and you will find rest for yourselves" (Matthew 11:28–29). The classic temptation for people in ministry is to diminish their own need to receive the ministry of others.

This requirement of receiving spiritual direction was the piece I

---

[19] See Mark 6:31–32; see also Luke 9:10. Jesus himself had a difficult time carving out space for quiet time alone: see Mark 3:20; Matthew 14:13.

resisted. Introverted by nature, I would much rather process things on my own—a good opportunity, no doubt, for the blind to lead the blind. But humbly I submitted myself to the wise counsel of another. Yet as the particular liturgical-vocational dimensions of my spiritual direction practice began to emerge, I found it increasingly difficult to find a spiritual director who could journey with me on this less traveled road. Directors in fact may encounter times when they will be unable to find a suitable director, or any director at all. The grace, I discovered, lies in knowing that it is God who leads us to those who can provide us with the rest, reflection, healing, and encouragement that we need. The spiritual director who seeks spiritual direction is blest indeed who encounters in a fellow director the invitation, challenge, and consolation of Jesus himself.

In those times when no suitable director can be found, the Lord himself becomes the soul's director—through the words of Scripture, through prayer and reflection, through discovery of unexpected spiritual oases.[20] In these times you may find yourself drawn through prayer to deeper *communio* in the Lord. You may find unusual openings of insight and an unexpected intimacy of prayer and the peace of indwelling in the Holy Spirit. We will explore the "directorless" times in more depth in Chapter 3.

---

[20] This situation is discussed in Nemeck and Coombs, *The Way of Spiritual Direction*, 52.

Bringing It Home

1. Whether I am a director or a directee, which of the seven core elements which serve as foundational pieces in the practice of spiritual direction most resonate with me? How so?

2. What can I say about my experience of prayer and my own engagement in prayer? How would I describe my experience of solitary prayer at this time? Does it adequately reflect where I am in my life now? Does my solitary prayer actually sustain me spiritually? If not, what needs to change?

3. How would I describe my experience of liturgical prayer? Has it become rote? Does it bring meaning and encouragement to my own experiences of dying, and hope for receiving new life?

Hold this Thought

I trust that the Lord Jesus himself is

the true director of my soul.

3

A MATCH MADE IN HEAVEN

Discerning the Right Director-Directee Relationship

"I have spent the last three years crawling across a spiritual desert," one directee confided at the start of our first conversation. "I have searched everywhere for a good spiritual director and was thinking that maybe I should give up the search—you know, just get over it, and get on with my life."

"Ah, God can work with this longing," I was thinking to myself even as this directee poured out her spiritual exhaustion. I knew intuitively what she soon discovered: God had been with her all along, leading her over the course of those three years through that spiritual desert, and had oriented her toward the horizon she was seeking. How did I know this?

I intuitively sensed that, even though we live in different states, indeed, different time zones, she had "arrived at my doorstep" for a purpose, and God indeed had led her to our working together—not because I am the answer to the soul's search for guidance but because she sighed an *unmistakable sigh of spiritual homecoming.*

How do you "find" the spiritual director who is right for you? In part, you may have to search. But equally important, you have to be open to being led. As the saying goes, "When the student is ready, the teacher will appear."[21] If God desires you to grow to full spiritual stature—and God does—then God will provide the guides, mentors, the trusted family member, or the Christian community, and all the necessary experiences and signposts to draw you to the full measure of your being-in-God.

In my own spiritual journey I have found myself in the desert places, seeking the guidance of one who could orient my soul and the many dimensions of my life in God's direction. I have had to live for long stretches with the ache of an unsatisfied search. The search itself can be an effective means of becoming clear about what you are actually hoping to find.

What, then, is the perfect match? It is the director-directee relationship that *God* desires. There is no one size that fits all. The deep work of spiritual and vocational direction is very particular, a relationship as fine-tuned in its unique expressions as the spousal relationship within a marriage. In its particular way, the director-directee relationship serves, on a smaller scale, the larger purpose of marriage: to aid the other in achieving spiritual wholeness and holiness.

Spiritual Husbandry

To place the search for a spiritual director in proper context, it helps if you can put into words what you are looking for. The particulars, of course, will vary. You may be looking for someone to help you to process anger or unforgiveness or grief. Or you may be looking for vocational guidance. You may want to grow deeper in prayer, or you may be looking for someone who can

---

[21] It is not unusual that a directee will say to me, "I can't exactly remember how I found you." Some have said, "I came across a Web site that had a link to another Web site. I don't know—I just followed the links." Finding the right spiritual director can be something like the experience of the Ethiopian eunuch who found Philip at the moment when he, unknowingly, was ready to understand the prophecy of Isaiah and to be baptized. Philip unexplainably appeared, and when the task was done, Philip equally unexplainably was whisked away (see Acts 8:26–40).

really hear what you need to say about a painful and defining life experience, help you to make sense of it, and take you seriously.

What the soul finally is searching for is what I will call "spiritual husbandry." This is not at all about a search for a "spiritual spouse" or spiritual marriage, or even a search for a soul companion. I am speaking here of something far more practical, far more—as the term implies—down to earth. Husbandry, a term often used in an agricultural context, refers to cultivating and caring for the land (or here, caring for the directee) in ways that make it easy for maximum fruitfulness to come about.

What does it mean for a spiritual director to "husband" the soul of the directee? It means, as the verb "husband" suggests, to tend to the soul, to tend (or attend) to its condition, to cultivate it, to ready it for the planting and harvesting seasons of a person's inner life. Spiritual husbandry is concerned with a loving and prudent care of the soul so that *God* can utilize its best qualities to greatest advantage. Spiritual husbandry has to do with cultivating the judicious use of the directee's spiritual resources, spiritual gifts, and natural abilities so that the directee becomes most fully available to the work of the Holy Spirit, the true Husband of the soul.

Many directees may not be able to describe their search for a spiritual or vocational director in terms of spiritual husbandry, and many directors may not be able to describe their practice in those terms, but in fact this tending of the soul of the other is the deepest and most engaging and vital work a spiritual and vocational director can do.

This givenness on the part of the director to the spiritual, relational, and vocational fruitfulness of the directee forms the basis for this relationship of extraordinary care and spiritual generosity.

As in husbandry of the land, its cattle and its crops, the spiritual director does not bring the authority of ownership but rather, the skill and humility of wise stewardship to the process of direction. Being something of a "farmer of the soul," the director strives to call forth the best interior conditions so that God can reap a plentiful harvest.

Discerning the Right Match

To even desire to receive spiritual or vocational direction is itself an indicator that God already has this deeply vital interior work in mind for you, and to some extent has already set this work in motion. But discerning this necessary interior work is different from discerning *who* God has in mind to guide you in this work. Indeed, every one of us is incapable of moving in God's direction apart from the grace to desire such movement and the guidance which gives strength of heart and sureness of foot. To revisit our opening question, "Are spiritual directors the next personal trainers?" the answer should be clear. Self-improvement for optimum performance is very different from tending to the interior growth that prepares you for the unglamorous and often humbling work of dying to self which is necessary to attain your full stature, your full fruitfulness, in Christ.[22]

Before you even begin to search for a spiritual director, you must hold in your heart a quiet trust that the right director will appear. The relationship does not start with you. It starts with God—specifically, with God's eternal and restless desire for your wholeness of life in Christ. The right director may be in your own parish, or across town. The right director may be across the continent. If God desires the two of you to work together, you will find each other. God's yearning within you for your wholeness of life is simply that powerful, that fruitful, and that perfect.[23]

---

[22] See Ephesians 4:13: "until we all attain to the unity of faith and knowledge of the Son of God ... to the extent of the full stature of Christ."

[23] Married couples have described their finding each other in similar terms, understanding that it was God's desiring that impelled them toward each other, sometimes across great distances and even across cultures.

Likewise, spiritual and vocational directors may wonder, "How should I advertise? How should I get my name out there? How will people find me?" And the same truth applies. If you indeed are gifted by the Holy Spirit for this particular work of love, and live the anointing of your calling with integrity and joy, then the people whom God desires to find you will find you. It is unexplainable and defies the logic of advertising and marketing plans. The spiritual director may hear directees say, "I don't really remember how I found you, or who gave me your name, or what Web site I searched. But here we are and I feel so grateful!"

But if this search for the right director turns up no leads, one of two things may be happening. First, you may be searching for "the perfect spiritual director." Every spiritual director I know would be the first to admit, "I am not perfect!" The search here can be something like the frustrating search for "the perfect spouse." (Variations on this theme can be the teenager's search for the perfect parents, and parents' search for the perfect teenager.) You see how pointless all of this searching becomes. "Perfect," in this sense, runs the risk of becoming an expression of spiritual narcissism.

Still, in God's design, there is a perfect director-directee relationship, oriented to the perfection of each—the director as well as the directee. The perfect director-directee relationship evokes honest self-reflection and self-revelation on the part of the directee, and equally evokes compassionate listening and wise discernment on the part of the director. In fact, it is not unusual that a directee's honest self-reflection inspires the director to be more attentive personally to this important discipline. The perfect spiritual and vocational director is not the one who affirms you in all the ways you want to be affirmed, nor the one who tells you all the things you want to hear. Rather, the perfection may be expressed in a loving patience, in fearlessly stepping with you into painful territory, in expression of compassion, or in readiness to defend your dignity and emotional space as the raw-edged shards of your life tumble out, exposed, unlovely, and worthy of respect.

Second, even if you are not searching for the "perfect" spiritual and vocational director and seek only the director whom God has in mind, your search may turn up no prospects. Why? Sometimes God may desire to lead you directly.[24] The point here, no matter the circumstances, is not to find a spiritual director but to move in God's direction. And that may mean moving *at* God's direction. As God assures us through the prophet Isaiah, "by paths unknown I will guide them" (Isaiah 42:16). This hidden way of God's guiding, even when no spiritual director appears, means that not having a director can never be an excuse for spiritual stagnation.

The shift of focus, from searching for a spiritual director to moving in God's direction, can occur without your knowing it. But great relief comes when you can intentionally let go a fruitless and frustrating search for the right director and discover that in the circumstances of your life God already has been directing your thoughts, your prayer, your understanding of things, your openness to unexpected possibility; already has been guiding you through difficult moral choices and a cleansing of heart, through the awkward conversations and the unrehearsed encounters. As soon as you find yourself feeling that your search for a spiritual or vocational director has become fruitless and frustrating, put down the paddle and coast gracefully in God's providence. God has no interest in your leaking away precious time, spirit, and strength by spinning in a closed loop of fruitlessness and frustration.

Indeed, fruitlessness and frustration are helpful indicators that it is now time for you to trust, and to let God actually be GOD in the circumstances of your life. By paths unknown God indeed will guide you. "I will not leave you orphans," Jesus tells his closest followers; "I will come to you" (John 14:18)—a powerful consolation which Jesus speaks in the context of his going away. But even here he does not leave us directionless. "I am the way" he assures his

---

[24] See Nemeck and Coombs, *The Way of Spiritual Direction,* 52. In St. Faustina's diary we read: "Know that it is a great grace on My part when I give a spiritual director to a soul. Many souls ask Me for this, but it is not to all that I grant this grace." See Sophia Michalenko, CMGT, *The Life of Faustina Kowalska: The Authorized Biography* (Cincinnati, OH: Servant Books/St. Anthony Messenger Press, 1999), 233–34.

followers (14:6).

In essence, the two guiding questions in your search for the "right" spiritual director are, first, "To whom is *God* desiring to send me for direction?" and second, if the director seems not to appear on your horizon, "How might God be guiding me directly?" When God is your director, the same honest self-reflection and self-revelation apply, along with faithfulness and obedience to this hidden way of direction. The same deep listening to the "tiny whispering sound"[25] of the Holy Spirit is still required of you—in the slow savoring of God revealed in Scripture, in the quiet intimacy of solitary prayer, in the dynamics of liturgical prayer, and in honest reflection on the circumstances of your life in light of Scripture and the church's heritage.

The Director's Discernment

Not every person who is seeking is at a place of readiness to enter into the formal relationship of spiritual and vocational direction. This is not at all to say that God is not desiring each person's growth into their fullness of personhood in Christ. Such divine desiring is a given. However, the director must play an important proactive role in discerning whether this particular director-directee relationship is in God's plan and in the directee's best interest. This proactive discernment is particularly important when the director, or the director's organization or community, benefits financially from the relationship.

Obstacles to readiness for this particular relationship can indeed exist— on the part of the directee as well as on the part of the director.

Some obstacles to readiness for the spiritual direction relationship which may manifest in the directee include:

---

[25] See 1 Kings 19:12. This passage can serve as an early biblical example of the soul being led by the Lord. Here the Lord God leads Elijah not in dramatic, thunderous, or otherwise obvious ways but by the gentlest whisper, as of the Spirit of God.

- an unwillingness to examine one's existential poverties,[26] those inner poverties that get in the way of authentic self-understanding;
- an undeveloped or misguided sense of God's calling in one's life, appearing sometimes as insurmountable unworthiness or, conversely, as a self-generated confidence in the "logical" or "obvious" vocational path;
- moral obstacles currently in one's life, or unresolved moral obstacles from one's past, that hinder honest self-reflection and self-revelation and therefore hinder openness to the guidance of the Holy Spirit through the director;
- an inability or unwillingness to integrate the seemingly disparate or inconsistent dimensions of one's life in light of God's deeper work;
- resistance to a prayer life commensurate with one's age and life circumstances.

None of this is to suggest that a directee has to achieve something close to spiritual perfection before engaging in spiritual or vocational direction. But certain thresholds of readiness must be in place so that the directee can authentically engage in and honor this unique spiritual relationship and submit to the scrutiny and grace of the Holy Spirit.

The director, too, may bring obstacles that prevent a full, wholehearted, and deeply engaged presence within the relationship. Obstacles here may include:

- unfinished inner work that prevents the director from working with certain topics or issues;
- an interior neediness to be known, accepted, or loved that seeks to elicit from the directee what the directee possibly cannot and certainly should not give;

---

[26] For an excellent meditation on the many poverties innate within the human experience, see the classic essay of Johannes Baptist Metz, *Poverty of Spirit* (translated by John Drury) (Mahwah, NJ: Paulist, 1968, 1998).

- an unwillingness to work with one's own existential poverties, thus frustrating the necessary work of dying to self and rising to new life in Christ which is the deep structure of Christian faith;
- moral obstacles that render the director incapable of perceiving the deeper content of the directee's words and the guidance of the Holy Spirit;
- distraction or preoccupation with other concerns, and careless preparation or lack of preparation for the scheduled encounter;
- resistance to a prayer life commensurate with the director's age, life circumstances, and calling to this ministry.

At the Heart of the Graced Relationship: Listening

Distinctively, the spiritual and vocational direction relationship is defined by a capacity to listen: director to directee, directee to director, and the capacity of the two together to listen to the Holy Spirit. In fact, the listening that goes on during the direction session ideally is an expression of the *habit* of listening within the director and directee that hopefully shapes the circumstances leading to this designated time of holy conversation. The *habit* of listening is the actual consistent orientation of the inner self toward the subtle promptings of the Holy Spirit—sometimes perceived as a hunch or intuition, and sometimes experienced as a stirring of heart or of conscience.

The quality of listening within the direction session reveals the capacity of each—director and directee—to listen intently and openly to "the innerness" of life's circumstances in those moments when life is happening. Tending lovingly to this capacity to listen, both on the part of the director and the directee, is the necessary work that enables the directee to move faithfully, trustingly, and confidently in God's direction in advance of the conversation and, beyond, when the conversation ends.

The fine-tuned listening which lies at the heart of the direction relationship is the same fine-tuned listening we hope to find at the heart of every authentic and intentional relationship. Real listening reveals a mature "capacity for the other"—whether that other is spouse, family member, dearest friend, neighbor, co-worker, fellow parishioner, or a complete stranger. Real listening is absolutely essential to real conversation (which is the opposite of, say, parallel monologues).

And real listening always involves a dying to self, a letting go of some of one's own words in order to create and defend a rightful and worthy space for the necessary words of the other. For people who like to move quickly to solutions and to action, real listening can oftentimes feel like a bother, an interruption or an obstacle to action, and a source of frustration. We will examine in detail the interior freedom required for real listening in chapter 11, "Integrating God's Movement."

The Directee's Discernment

Certainly the director has an obligation to discern whether God is actually desiring this particular director-directee relationship to come about. But the potential directee also has an important work of discernment. Jesus speaks a word of warning that serves as a worthy caution in discerning the right director-directee match: "Can a blind person guide a blind person? Will not both fall into a pit?" (Luke 6:39). How can a potential directee discern whether this possible director possesses clear, Christ-centered interior vision? Here are some valuable questions which any potential directee should feel free to ask, and which any Christ-centered director should be able to clearly and convincingly answer:

- *Can you tell me about your prayer life?* As a potential directee, listen for evidence of a rhythm of prayer, and steadfast adherence to a life of prayer that bespeaks a living relationship with the living Christ. Listen, too, for evidence of a variety of types of prayer, especially liturgical prayer (as discussed in chapter 2 under point 6, "Commitment to Prayer") and contemplative styles of prayer (including *lectio divina* or extended sitting with Scripture).

- *What qualifies you to be a spiritual director?* Listen for the quality and depth of training received for the practice of spiritual direction. Listen, too, for *evidence* of other training, education, and formation in the theological foundations of Christ-centered spiritual life. Perhaps most important, ask for examples of how the director capably integrates these many disciplines within the spiritual direction practice.
- *What mix of spiritual gifts do you bring to your practice?* Listen here for convincing evidence, including examples, of the following charisms:
  - *Encouragement,* or the capacity to invite honest conversation on the *troubling* or diminished or suppressed aspects of a person's life, and the ability to bring strength of heart and unexpected hope to the other, through presence, listening, and words. *Opposites* of Encouragement could be impatience, superficial cheerleading, or interrupting the directee's narrative to share one's own story.
  - *Wisdom,* or the capacity to quickly and accurately get a sense of the larger context or perceive the whole of a situation, and the unusual ability to quickly and accurately identify or diagnose the piece that does not fit or that needs to be addressed in practical ways. The *opposite* of Wisdom could be having a "tin ear," an inability to know where to go with what has just been said, or jumping to solutions out of a desire to be helpful.
  - *Evangelism,* or the capacity to quickly and accurately perceive how another is ready to be awakened to a more mature relationship with Jesus and with the church. The *opposite* of Evangelism could be hesitancy toward addressing the directee's quality of living faith for fear of being "pushy," or, conversely, delivering a blunt-edge battering with guilt-inducing "should" language.

As a directee seeking to discern the right director, ask clear questions and do not be afraid to probe. Some very well intentioned people may mistakenly perceive themselves as spiritual directors when the necessary foundations and gifts are not there. Others may be presumed by outsiders to be spiritual directors because of their title, position, or role within an institution.

Still, some people are "natural spiritual directors" who would never seek the title or the position, and have never had the formal training, but who seem consistently to be unusually effective channels of God's grace, wisdom, encouragement, and love to the people they meet. They seem to be capable of honest conversation that leads others to real spiritual growth.

As a directee in search of the director whom God has in mind for you, ask and do not assume that just because this particular director has appeared on your horizon, this is the one whom God has in mind. Be aware of your needs, your hopes, and your expectations. But also be aware that your hopes and expectations might be too small for what God has in mind for your life. God may be desiring to move you in ways and directions you had not imagined, or to address wounds and incapacities you would rather keep hidden. Discerning the right director is not a guessing game. You are God's well-beloved, and God takes your life seriously. Allow the Holy Spirit to lead the way and confirm the relationship.

Next we will explore the four commitments that shape the heart of the director-directee relationship.

Bringing It Home

1.Given where I am presently in my spiritual journey, what qualities would the "perfect" spiritual director possess? And why do I perceive *these* qualities as perfect for me at this time?

2.Am I searching for the perfect spiritual director (or perhaps perfection in my current director)? Or am I doing the more challenging work of actually moving in God's direction—with or without a perfect director? How so, or in what ways?

Hold this Thought

I am "turning down the volume" in my life

in order to better hear what the Holy Spirit desires to communicate.

4

NAVIGATING THE
DIRECTOR-DIRECTEE RELATIONSHIP

Four Mutual Commitments

Whether you are the director or the directee, once you have discerned and begun to trust that the Holy Spirit is desiring this particular holy conversation to commence, the real work of direction begins. Yet this "work" is not first about things to be done but about a relationship to be entered into.

From the outset both director and directee will do well to let go agendas —especially the director's age-old temptation to identify a problem and fix it, and the directee's age-old temptation to present a problem that needs to be fixed. In reality, many people seek spiritual or vocational direction because they feel that they have come to a stuck point in their life, or find themselves in a holding pattern, or at a Y in the road; or sometimes they feel just plain lost.

But the point of spiritual and vocational direction is not first and foremost to solve problems or to come to a clear, clinical understanding of the nature or origins of problems, but to bring the directee into a more authentic, dynamic, and spiritually fruitful relationship with self, God, and the world. In the process of spiritual and vocational direction problems may become resolved, but the real dynamic at work in spiritual and vocational direction is movement through—not around but *through*—the stuck points and uncertainties in order to give oneself to more authentic life in Christ. This is the point of Christ-centered spiritual and vocational direction.

Whether the spiritual direction relationship is face-to-face, via phone, or through the back-and-forth of e-mails, it is, at heart, a relationship—two people in meaningful and caring dialogue, focused not so much on each other as on the Mystery at work in this holy conversation and in the spaces between the words, the holy silences. This is a relationship focused on the mystery of God's presence and God's desiring, the mystery of the Holy Spirit at work in hidden and sure ways in the life of this particular beloved one of God.

The director-directee relationship, like every authentic relationship, requires some commitments mutually expressed between the parties. What are these mutual commitments?

The Four Commitments

The first commitment is to *humility,* and to expanding one's capacity to recognize that, apart from God, one possesses nothing and controls nothing. Equally for director and directee, humility requires the willingness to acknowledge that all fruits of this privileged relationship flow from the Holy Spirit in cooperation with each of them and both of them together. As director, I may experience humility in realizing that God has chosen me to enter onto the sacred ground of this other person's anguish, trials, morally complex circumstances, and yearning for something in life that is worthy of wholehearted commitment.

As directee, I may experience humility in letting go the carefully constructed façade and in entrusting to another my life's confusions, complexities, and sometimes my stupid or hurtful choices—in short, exposing the interior wound to the light of God's healing grace.

The second mutual commitment within the director-directee relationship is to *honesty,* and to expanding one's capacity to speak the truth. To express honesty means to honor or to hold in worthy esteem the truth of one's being-in-God, to honor one's self-worth which lies beyond the horizons of personal imagination. Concurrently, honesty means to gently hold one's existential poverties and accept them for what they are—portals into encounter with God. As director, I may express honesty in sharing with the directee the graced and sometimes sobering but liberating insight I have found hidden deep within a seemingly insignificant word or phrase, a tone, a gesture, a dismissive laugh, or a burdened sigh which the directee has shared. Honesty can never be used as a cover for emotional or spiritual brutality; rather, in the context of this holy conversation honesty is more like the surgeon's delicate scalpel used deftly, precisely, and sparingly. Honesty expressed in the director, and which generates from the Holy Spirit, brings with it its twin, which is mercy, which defends and affirms the dignity of the other.

As a directee I may express honesty by allowing the Holy Spirit to direct my understanding of the circumstance I am bringing to the light of this holy conversation—even though I may have thought about or even wrestled with this circumstance and even come to some premature conclusions. I express honesty by allowing the Holy Spirit to place on my tongue words I had not thought of saying, giving witness to Jesus' promise: "For the holy Spirit will teach you at that moment what you should say" (Luke 12:12). Honesty in the directee rests upon an underlying foundation of trust, or "entrustment," which allows the directee to fully believe that the director will receive these words reverently, with an understanding heart, and will defend their capacity to express what needs to be said.

The third mutual commitment within the director-directee relationship is to *obedience,* which means, in essence, to listen with the interior ear, the ear of the heart, and to act accordingly. Surprising as this may sound, as director I am called to obedience to this relationship. As director, I am the foot washer, the servant. Therefore, as director I express obedience in my relationship to this directee by creating space interiorly for this unique individual, this particular one who is beloved of God, whether I experience satisfaction from our conversation or feel impatient or even repulsed. At a deeper level I may express obedience as a "leaning into" the words of the directee, being intentionally engaged and fully present, even when this leaning into the other's words is a sheer act of will.

As a directee I may experience obedience as an act of discipling, entering into stillness in certain moments in the course of the conversation in order to learn what God desires to teach me and to be more deeply formed in mind and heart and spirit. Obedience, as a disciple's act of listening for God's willing, becomes the means by which each of us is conformed to Christ.[27] In both director and directee, obedience is a surrender of personal will and understanding in service to the Holy Spirit who is the real director within this holy relationship. In the surrender, the letting go, both director and directee become free to experience a simplicity of heart which invites outcomes beyond what could be expected in ordinary or even therapeutic conversation.

Finally, the fourth mutual commitment within the director-directee relationship is to *love* (or *caritas*)—to encounter the other as God encounters the other. This expression of love which is true charity—which in essence means "true costliness"—enables the two to enter into a spiritual *communio* which is a foretaste of the divine indwelling for which Jesus ardently prayed in his final discourse on the night before his own costly self-offering.[28] This love, or *caritas,* or *communio,* may initially express itself as feelings of encouragement and hope. But more deeply, this love, or *caritas,* or *communio,* is a stirring of the

---

[27] See Romans 8:29: "For those he foreknew he also predestined to be conformed to the image of his Son"; Romans 12:2: "Do not conform yourself to this age but be transformed by the renewal of your mind"; and Philippians 3:10: "to know him and the power of his resurrection and [the] sharing of his sufferings by being conformed to his death, if somehow I may attain the resurrection of the dead."

[28] See John 17:20–24: "I pray … for those who will believe in me … that they may all be one, as you, Father, are in me and I in you."

Holy Spirit as director and directee begin to encounter the living Christ himself in the depths of heart speaking to heart.[29] This spiritual *communio* between director and directee is a micro-expression of Christian community fed on the presence and delight of the risen Lord himself.

As director, by love's authority at work within me I experience a genuine caring for the soul, the life, and the destiny of this particular directee. Impelled by love I apprentice myself to the discipline of learning the tender care of the Shepherd for this particular lamb. I apprentice myself to the pastoral care and spiritual husbandry born of the love which flows from the heart of God.

As directee, through a steadfast commitment to love, I begin to experience an authentic or deeper expression of self-love and expression of my own self-worth as a beloved one of God. I may begin to experience a sense of the dignity of my own personhood powerful enough to call me forth toward the full flowering and fruitbearing of my own life in ways which only the divine Mystery of love can do.

Among these four mutual commitments, we can see humility, honesty, and obedience as the simple yet powerful means to open up and animate the director-directee relationship. And love? Love is the vocational piece. Love evokes, calls forth, imparts the unique identity of one's personhood in God. Love animates, engages, and sustains not only director and directee, but the mystery of relationship which has drawn them together and gives them an interior longing to fully realize the fruits that come from moving in God's direction.

Terminating the Relationship

---

[29] Something of this same stirring of the Holy Spirit was expressed in the greeting of the young virgin Mary upon entering the home of Zechariah to greet her kinswoman Elizabeth. See Luke 1:39–45.

If God has called this relationship into being, then both director and directee must carefully examine the underlying reasons for desiring to terminate it. The director-directee relationship is not a marriage; it is not a "forever" commitment. But it also is not a commodity of convenience. Because spiritual and vocational direction is oriented toward guiding individuals in their lifelong work of moving in God's direction, it cannot be compared to, say, a yearlong membership at the gym. It is a living, breathing entity requiring of both director and directee a wholehearted humility, honesty, obedience, and love—all elements that are essential to every real and worthy relationship.

So when should—or does—the spiritual and vocational direction relationship end? Let's look at some key indicators.

The relationship may become seriously wounded and subject to review. Such wounding occurs when either director or directee:

- replaces humility with a sense of self-sufficiency, off-handedness, complacency, or repeated casual unpreparedness or inattention;
- chooses untruthfulness or concealment over honesty, even if such concealment is regarded as a way to "not offend" the other;
- resists obedience to the Holy Spirit and the deeper working of the Holy Spirit in either the director or the directee;
- offends or dismisses or betrays the love or *communio* which is a celebration of the Lord who is the unseen Presence at the heart of the relationship.

Beyond situations which wound the relationship, other reasons exist, too, for ending the relationship. The director may move, retire from practice, experience loss of health or other change in life circumstances which render the director unavailable or unable to be fully present to the directee. The directee may have similar logistical or circumstantial reasons for ending the director-directee relationship.

The director and directee may discern—sometimes one sooner than the other—that the relationship is not working, and that the Holy Spirit for some reason is not present—or not free to be present—in the dynamic way hoped for at the outset. Perhaps some solitary interior work needs to be accomplished within one or the other before the work of spiritual direction can fruitfully continue.

God is not capricious with our lives, so separation due to a lack of "fit" may indicate to the director that a deeper or more thorough or honest process of discernment was needed at the outset. Or a "lack of fit" may tell the director that the directee is pushing back from a threshold of discovery and growth—in other words, may be resisting the difficult but necessary next step on the path to fullness of personhood. Or the lack of fit may have to do with the director not being professionally qualified or spiritually gifted to address the concerns of this particular directee.

A director may strive either subtly or overtly to keep a directee who seems ready to terminate, simply to avoid a sense of failure or to escape a feeling of professional or vocational incompetence. For some directors the volume of directees might bolster a belief that "people need me" or that "I must be good at what I do—maybe even better than my colleagues who don't have as many directees." Boastfulness, or a "puffed up spirit,"[30] is the real enemy here, and at all times to be guarded against by the expression of genuine love. And while spiritual and vocational direction is not a "commodity," to the director who receives a stipend or fee for services the prospect of a drop in income can feel threatening.

Directees too may wish to terminate the relationship. The directee may feel that "now that my problem has been fixed" there is no real need to continue spiritual and vocational direction. In our hurry-up world the challenge for both director and directee is to defend a worthy space for this holy conversation to continue beyond the boundaries of an isolated problem or vocational concern, and to expand outward toward the broader and unexplored horizons of personhood. Such broader work honors the mystery of a life that is moving in

---

[30] See 1 Corinthians 4:6, 18–19.

God's direction, allowing that divine movement to unfold organically, richly, and fully.

The pace of relationship certainly may change over time. The directee may sense that a major chunk of spiritual work has been accomplished, and may be ready for less frequent meetings. When this indeed is the case, the director will share that sense, and the two will become free to adjust the frequency of their meetings accordingly.

The directee may discover that the Holy Spirit is leading the way to a different director. On first blush, the directee may feel like "I've outgrown my current director" and begin to diminish or even disdain the gift and merit of the relationship. What often is the case is that the directee may now be ready for growth beyond the director's capabilities or outside the director's core areas of focus. Spiritual directors are not God; they come with their unique mix of gifts, experiences, insights, methods, and directional focus. If the directee really is being led by the Holy Spirit to another director, the discernment of termination will bring a mutual peace and blessing.

But something else can motivate the directee to terminate the relationship and search for a new director. The directee may resent the way the Holy Spirit, through the current director, has such a precise and challenging way of "hitting the nail on the head." Director-hopping because the directee is not pleased with the direction in which the conversation is moving is not at all the same as being led by the Holy Spirit to the care of another director. Director-hopping, or opting out of spiritual direction altogether, is a unilateral decision, not a shared discernment, and brings unsettled feelings rather than a sense of peace in both the director and the directee.

What has been given as a gift—namely, this unique relationship of holy conversation—must be mutually guarded and tended and cherished as a gift. Humility, honesty, obedience, and love assign the director and the directee, each in their own ways, as the trusted stewards of this conversational encounter with the living Christ.

Bringing It Home

1. Whether I am a director or a directee, what role does *humility* play in my direction relationship? How do I actually express humility? What examples come to mind?

2. In this relationship, when have I expressed *honesty* when I easily could have held back, played it safe, and been less candid? How did my honesty affect the conversation?

3. When have I expressed obedience, or a "listening heart," in the direction relationship? What has that been like for me?

4. In what specific ways do I express *love* (or *caritas*) in the spiritual direction relationship? What instances come to mind? How has expression of *caritas* shaped the relationship?

Hold this Thought

Increasingly I cherish the direction relationship

as a real treasure.

WHY IN THE WORLD DOES SPIRITUAL AND VOCATIONAL DIRECTION MATTER?

A Look from Three Perspectives

Let's go back to that opening contrast between spiritual and vocational direction and working with a personal trainer. When you work with the personal trainer, what happens when your life gets busy, or your finances tighten, or you have achieved a suitable state of buff? That personal trainer may not seem quite as useful as when you first took on your fitness regimen.

But spiritual and vocational direction is quite different from working with a personal trainer. It is not that as a directee you will never be "perfect" (we could say "spiritually buff"). Rather, as you mature, your life circumstances draw you only more deeply into the divine Mystery, the mystery of God. So you will discover that your ongoing pursuit of spiritual and vocational direction becomes increasingly important not only to you, but to God who is fully invested in you, and increasingly important to the world which you touch. We will take a look at all three of these perspectives in light of what it means to be moving in God's direction.

The Self Moving Toward God

I personally am far too lazy to ever submit my body to the rigors of a personalized physical fitness regimen. The parts of me that most need the attention and disciplines of a personal trainer would rebel instinctively. I simply will not put my body through such anguish.

But moving in God's direction, both immediately and toward a more distant horizon, is about ultimate things. The fitness of my soul matters everlastingly. It also matters in my dealings with others here and now. Even more immediately, moving in God's direction matters in my moral choice making, in my attitude toward life and my life's circumstances, and in my relationships with those closest to me and with those who are passing strangers. Why? Because by virtue of my baptism into Christian life I am anointed to be the presence of the risen Lord in my particular place in this world.

The self moving in God's direction is an anointed self. And this anointing is no transitory event but "an indelible spiritual mark" of your "belonging to Christ."[31] As we move more surely in God's direction we discover that "belonging to Christ" is all-encompassing. In fact, belonging to Christ will require our giving over of our total self, and eventually will claim every dimension of our lives. St. Teresa of Avila, the sixteenth century Spanish Carmelite reformer, writes more bluntly:

> Do you know when people really become spiritual? It is when they become the slaves of God and are branded with His sign, which is the sign of the Cross, in token that they have given him their freedom. Then He can sell them as slaves to the whole world, as He Himself was sold, and if He does this He will be doing them no wrong but showing

---

[31] *Catechism of the Catholic Church,* Second Edition, English Translation (Washington, DC: U.S. Catholic Conference, 1994, 1997) (hereafter *CCC*), para. 1272.

them no slight favor.[32]

These words echo what St. Paul wrote repeatedly in his letters to the early churches: Your life is not your own, you are Christ's; you have been purchased, and at what price? Your life now is hidden in Christ.[33]

Unlike membership in a club, where you have status as long as you pay your dues, in Baptism your "status" is sealed everlastingly in the Holy Spirit—that dynamic yet hidden force of God's love which renders your life ultimately fruitful.

Which is to say that you must be present and actively engaged in your own life. Your life work is to partner with the Holy Spirit in becoming your authentic self whom God has desired all along. Jesus is piercingly clear in his words to one of the scribes, a scholar of the law: "You shall love the Lord your God with *all* your heart, with *all* your soul, with *all* your mind, and with *all* your strength" (Mark 12:30, emphasis added). In short, every dimension of your life demands your wholeheartedness in God's service. Every dimension of your life is anointed to be the living, breathing, Spirit-filled presence of the risen Lord. For the good of others, yes, and concurrently for your own growth in holiness, which really means growth in God.

Why would spiritual and vocational direction matter to you? You are on that path to holiness which is *your* path, untrod by any other, a path that is never fully revealed even to you. When you hear yourself saying hopefully, "Let's see what tomorrow brings," you are confessing a core limitation in your being human: You do not know what immediate turn or larger trajectory your path to holiness will take. You may have a hunch, but that hunch is very, very different from obediently and faithfully putting one foot in front of the other today, here

---

[32] See Kieran Kavanaugh, OCD, and Otilio Rodriguez, OCD, translators, *The Collected Works of St. Teresa of Avila, Vol. II* (Washington, DC: ICS, 1980), 446–447. This translation was taken from Teresa of Avila, *Interior Castle,* "Seventh Mansions," chap. 4, para. 8 (http://www.catholictreasury.info/books/interior_castle/ic31.php, accessed December 10, 2011).

[33] See 1 Corinthians 6:20, "For you have been purchased at a price"; and Colossians 3:3: "For you have died, and your life is hidden with Christ in God."

and now.

Why Your Direction Matters: A Personal Perspective

When my friend Mary approached me in the church parking lot those many years ago and urged me to pursue studies in spiritual direction, I resisted. It wasn't because I did not want to become a spiritual director. Quite honestly, I had not given it any thought.[34] I resisted formation as a spiritual director because I resisted submitting myself to the wise and caring guidance of another person concerning the circumstances of my own life. At the root of it all, I did not understand why in the world it would matter whether I received such guidance or not.

And that's the operative phrase that holds the key: Why *in the world.* Spiritual and vocational direction is only partly about "me." Neither you nor I live our lives in a social vacuum. We touch the world constantly, and are touched by the world. Think of your work life, the people you encounter daily—co-workers or colleagues; maybe customers, clients, students, patients, or patrons whom you serve; maybe face-to-face, maybe by phone or Internet. Others encounter you through the words you speak publicly, the works you have written, the things you have created. Think of the people you touch in your family life—inlaws, outlaws, siblings, venerable aunties, favorite cousins, black sheep who show up at Christmas, your teenaged or young adult children and their strange and fascinating friends.

All of these relationships and the emotional complexities and moral challenges that you encounter in them are worthy of the wise and caring guidance of spiritual direction.

---

[34] Later I realized that becoming a spiritual director was the desire I could not name twenty years earlier when, in graduate studies in theology, I had hoped to create a position as "confessional counselor" at a retreat center for women. At that time I could not find a better or a more accurate name for the one-to-one work I desired to do. I felt drawn to helping women to process the deeper issues and identify the meaning-making context for the matters they would bring to the sacrament of Reconciliation.

Spiritual and vocational direction matters because the quality of your living, the integrity of your moral choice making, and the clarity of your commitments in this confused and complex world are always at stake, always up for grabs by darker forces. Day after day, sometimes minute by minute, as the weight of your world presses in, it is easy to lose your focus, and to forget in the heat of the moment that everything, *everything,* begs to be seen, encountered, and expressed through the lens of the Gospel. The imperative to love with the heart of Jesus and to sort out wheat from chaff with the wisdom of the Holy Spirit is ever before you. The imperative to believe, in the midst of overwhelming world anguish, that all things indeed do hold together in Christ[35] will press your heart and your imagination to the frighteningly thin line between hope and despair, or at least between hope and profound discouragement.

The world you touch, through familial and social and workplace relationships, may be looking to you more than you realize for clues about how to be human, alive, and authentically present in a world of excess, deprivation, and moral confusion. The work of spiritual direction can help you to focus with grace, with insight, and with laserlike precision on the challenges you face, the gifts you bring, and the often surprising opportunities to orient yourself more fully in God's direction.

Indeed, spiritual and vocational direction is about moving in God's direction. The vocational dimension is inseparable from the spiritual, just as the global is inseparable from the personal. "If [one] part suffers, all the parts suffer with it," St. Paul writes (1 Corinthians 12:26). The familiar phrase, "When you are wounded, I bleed," finds its sobering origins in the self-offering of the crucified Lord. Moving in God's direction is not merely about you moving in your private spiritual life toward God, but you *moving in your world with God* and you *moving your world toward God.* All of your relationships, your commitments, and your presence through your many forms of engagement with your world, all your loves, your hopes, your passion—all of this has been given to you so that you can move it all, knowingly or by hidden grace, toward God

---

[35] See Colossians 1:17.

and into God.

Why in the world, why in *your* world, would your engagement in spiritual and vocational direction matter? It matters because you have been anointed as a co-participant in God's mighty work of redemption, a work much larger than yourself that will require the engagement of all your heart, all your soul, all your mind, and all your strength. Your anointing for participation in such a worthy mission is the source of your dignity.

Why Your Direction Matters: God's Perspective

Now we can ask the same question from a second perspective: Why in the world would spiritual and vocational direction—specifically, your active engagement in the spiritual and vocational direction of your life—matter to God? Does God really care whether you tend to the maturing of your inner life in this manner? *Yes, of course,* we intuitively reply. Yet what is the evidence?

When I initially dragged my feet at the prospect of pursuing spiritual direction, both as director and directee, God did not smite me for my resistance. In fact, I heard nothing from God. (Truth be told, I did not consult with God, either. I found it easier to hide, at least for a while, than to bring the topic to prayer.) Nor will God smite you if you resist God's invitation to spiritual and vocational growth. God is not interested in smiting people. We do a good enough job of smiting ourselves.

But God is passionately interested in relationship, in being the unfathomable and ever luring "Thou" to your "I." In fact, Jesus prayed for us an even more intimate relationship than "I and Thou." On the night of his arrest Jesus prayed "that they may all be one, as you, Father, are in me and I in you, that they also may be in us, that the world may believe that you sent me" (John 17:21). In this most spiritually intimate language we hear Jesus praying for us not an I-and-Thou relationship *with* God but an intimate indwelling, I-in-Thou. And he includes in this prayer the connective phrase: *that the world may believe.*

Our experience of divine indwelling is not for our personal consolation alone. From God's perspective this divine indwelling, I-in-Thou, necessarily pulses outward through us in embrace of the world.

God's passion, expressed in this eloquent and deeply felt prayer of Jesus, is for our vocational fulfillment: life in God, which by its very nature presses outward so that the world we touch and inhabit will be touched, deeply touched and even transformed, by the indescribable good of this relationship of divine-human indwelling. The evidence that God passionately cares that you become fully engaged in your spiritual and vocational maturing is that God already is fully invested in you—in the life, death, and resurrection of Jesus, the well-beloved Son. As St. Paul writes: "He who did not spare his own Son but handed him over for us all, how will he not also give us everything else along with him?" (Romans 8:32).

Your similarly passionate investment in your spiritual and vocational destiny is not one option among many. The circumstances of *your* life constitute the path uniquely given to you by which you come to fullness of personhood, fullness of self-in-God. You do not choose this path; it is given uniquely to you with great love and inscrutable wisdom. Even the fervent passion with which you journey on your path is not your own. This passion that fuels your journey is also gift, a portion of the flame that burns within the heart of God. The moving force within you which impels you to move in God's direction—whether you know it or not—is the Holy Spirit. God indeed is passionately invested in the spiritual and vocational trajectory of your life.

Why Your Direction Matters: The World's Perspective

Now comes the more challenging question: What compelling reason does your world have to care whether you engage in spiritual and vocational direction for your life? What *in the world* has actually changed, or is changing, or likely will change, because you enter regularly into deep and holy conversation with another about the things that matter most to you? Does the *world* care whether you work your way through grief, through a moral stuck point, through anger, through unfinished business, through a messy relationship, through career failure, through a burden of guilt, through the stone wall of unforgiveness, through an unquenchable thirst for God? Does the *world you touch* care whether you gain clarity on the ways in which God is calling and anointing you to be the presence of the living Christ? Would your world even notice?

Most of us live much of our life on a fairly local scale. Like Jesus in his hidden years, we live for the most part "in Nazareth."[36] Our worlds extend maybe to the borders of our town, with some tendrils reaching out to those places where family and old acquaintances live. If our work involves travel, our world may extend up and down the county or across the state, or even to select cities across the nation. The small pebbles of our daily commitments and life experience are oftentimes just that—pebbles, and their ripples can be graceful and somewhat short range. As we engage in our various communities of love and concern and civic life some of our collective pebbled circles of presence touch; some circles of love and concern overlap. Sometimes the ripples become lost in the rush of rapids of unexpected circumstances and unbidden change.

The truth is, every one of us inhabits a world of relationships and commitments, engagements and meanings. We gravitate toward communities of meaning, and sometimes we even generate communities of meaning. Our lives are woven together by invisible threads of divine grace and holy possibility. And we discover that "our world" is not just something out there but is a part of us. We are threaded together whether we know each other's name or not. It's not so much about knowing each other's name as it is regarding each other with a divine and tender care that holds our common world together.[37] The quality of

---

[36] For a lovely description of this experience of "living in Nazareth," see the essay on Charles de Foucauld in Robert Ellsberg, *All Saints: Daily Reflections on Saints, Prophets, and Witnesses for Our Time* (New York: Crossroad, 1997, 2010), 524–25.

[37] This forging of communities is found in spinoffs of the Occupy movement throughout the United States which seek to engage citizens in authentic conversation on the social and therefore moral dimensions of governance, commerce, community, and the common good.

your life matters. The grace and integrity with which you live your life matters, both now and everlastingly. Why? Because the grace and integrity with which you live your life starts not with you but finds its origin in the very heart of God, and reaches outward to the world you touch. The world is your means of experiencing in your time and circumstances the astonishing reality of the Incarnation.

People may not see or perceive the good you bring. Or they may intuit the good which is at work but not be able to name it. Or, they might see it and perceive it but reject it. Jesus was surrounded by people who were slow to understand. He encountered outright rejection over the unnamable authority of his teaching, and he was accused of blasphemy for his words of forgiveness and for his works of healing, compassion, and scandalously inclusive table fellowship. The grace and integrity with which you live your life and touch your world might convince only a handful of people of God's goodness present in personal and redeeming ways here and now. Organizationally, that is all Jesus seemingly managed to do. But from that first unimpressive handful of followers has come a mighty throng.

So the question now becomes personal, and boils down to this: Why, for the sake of the world you touch, would you pursue spiritual and vocational direction? Why, for the sake of your world and the times in which you live, would you seek to move your life in God's direction?

You might do it because it seems like the right and clarifying thing to do. What you will eventually discover is that the more you seek to move in God's direction, the closer you come to being incapable of *not* moving in God's direction.

The Holy Spirit waits at every moment for the unrestricted freedom to be the animator of your life's mission, accomplishing *in* you and *through* you what eye has not yet seen and ear has not yet heard, and what has not yet entered the human heart, the unimaginable good that God has prepared for those who love him.[38]

---

[38] See 1 Corinthians 2:9.

Bringing It Home

1. In my own experience, what has moved me—or what *is* moving me, or might soon move me—to seek spiritual direction? What is the motivator here? How can I best describe it?

2. What evidence do I have that my pursuit of spiritual and vocational direction matters to God? Has spiritual and vocational direction sharpened my practice of moving in God's direction?

3. How has my engagement in spiritual and vocational direction made a difference in the ways I engage in the concerns in my world? Or if I am not there yet, how might such direction affect the ways I engage in the concerns of my world?

Hold this Thought

I am becoming more fully engaged in this life

in which God is fully invested.

Part II

THE MATURING CONVERSATION

The Spiritual Meets the Vocational

In Part I we have explored how moving in God's direction is essential to growth toward fullness of personhood in Christ—not merely for the sake of personal holiness but for the sake of this world which God still so loves.

In Part II we will examine the intersection of the spiritual with the vocational and the ways in which spiritual fruitfulness is expressed in your life and in your world.

6

GOD MEETS ME WHERE I AM

A Look at Vocational Lifestyle

A strange feeling came over me the other evening during the seasonal Penance Service. As people waited quietly in the softly lighted church for their turn in the confessional, I looked around and saw faces looking downward, eerily lighted by the blue-green glow of their iPhones. Scrolling, scrolling, scrolling, what were they looking for? I consoled myself with the thought that maybe they were not checking for messages; maybe they were looking up the Penitential psalms, or searching for a prayer for a worthy confession. Still, I had the feeling that I was surrounded by people who were here, yes, but really somewhere else.

Communications technology today, even though wireless for the most part, has pretty much "hardwired" us to be somewhere else, with cell phones, text messaging, tweeting, friending, and who knows what else. Real conversation, the kind of conversation that can get to the heart of a matter, never has been a goal of social networking, so this curious form of "connecting" oftentimes is not so much social as it is an obstacle to being authentically present, one self to another. Rather, today's social networking seems to be a means of "communication" that often only adds to an interior restlessness—a restlessness that agitates all the way down to the core of one's being, an existential loneliness that might eventually shape who we are as a society and determine where we stand: a community, of sorts, of the isolated.

Where Are You, Anyway?

In the Book of Genesis, after the Fall, God asks the man, "Where are you?" (3:9). It appears to be a simple enough question. But what we intuitively understand in this passage is that you never want God, the great I AM, the ever-present One, whose middle name is Relationship, to have to go in search of you. God does not care what aisle of the supermarket you are in, or where you are in the parking structure, or whether you are just about to board your flight. When God—or your spiritual director—asks, "Where *are* you?" it is an existential question, a spiritual question, a vocational question in search of an authentic self. It is, in the end, the one question you never want God, personally, to ask of you.

How do you move from technologically "being somewhere else" to existentially "being here now"? This is the urgently pressing spiritual question for our times. Technologically, the ease of being "connected" with someone or something somewhere else is rapidly becoming the malaise of disconnection from this particular present moment which God is giving you for a purpose right now. How *do* you be here now—fully, authentically, wholeheartedly? In a word, the answer is simple: eliminate the distractions and notice, notice, notice.[39] God asks "Where are you?" not in order to be in control, but to be in relationship.

The antidote to *distraction* (which means to be drawn apart, pulled apart, confused) is *presence* (which means to be attendant before another, or attendant to the circumstances at hand). The intentional act of noticing your

---

[39] I think here of a bumper sticker I have seen around town: "Hang up and drive."

circumstances has an awakening and a magnetic-like effect, freeing you to be present to what's happening here and now. Noticing your circumstances enables you to be accountable and engaged. How do you develop the practice of being intentionally present to the circumstances at hand? The steps are not complex.

For starters, turn off the electronic gizmos and notice your surroundings and your circumstances.[40] It is perfectly OK, as you wait at the gate for your flight, to notice the cloud formations across the sky. It is OK, as you wait for your next appointment, or for your turn in line, to notice the people around you, to imagine their world, and to lift them up in prayer. Let go the techno toys and notice the gift, the invitation (often vocational), or the challenge of this particular day. When the tasks of your day, or even your entire life circumstances, seem to be going nowhere or even going against you, you can ask yourself: "Where is God in this? Where am I *with* God in this?" Allow these questions to draw you into worthy conversation with the more hidden or even perplexing dimensions of your life. Your honest answers to these questions hold the power to spring you out of the imprisonment of self-preoccupation—or even benign narcissism—and set you free to be your authentic self-in-God.

The Vocational Dimension of Noticing

Actually noticing the circumstances of your life, being present and wholeheartedly engaged, is important spiritual work. Being intentionally present to your life is a key prerequisite to living a fully human life and, for the baptized man or woman, is absolutely essential to living a vocationally authentic life. *How* you engage in your world, through your gifts, your talents, and your perceptions and ways of making meaning, is a key indicator of who God is calling you to be in this world. The particular ways in which you wholeheartedly engage in your world are both clues and an affirmation of your vocational lifestyle. What does this mean?

---

[40] When I take walks, especially on the nearby university campus, I often wonder if most people would notice, or even care, if the birds stopped singing, or worse, simply went away.

God's calling in your life is not first of all to *do something*, but to *be interiorly awake* and to *be someone*. God's calling first of all is for you to wake up to the person whom God has desired you to be from all eternity. The *way* you live your life and express your unique personhood in God is called your "vocational lifestyle," which you live specifically through *singlehood,* or through *Christian marriage,* or through *celibate life*—each expressing relationship to God and to others in very particular ways. Let's examine each of these terms.[41]

As a Christian vocational lifestyle, *single* means, simply, not married but open to dating and to the possibility of marriage—specifically, open to the sacramental life of Christian marriage. *Married* means living in a consecrated perpetual, exclusive, intimate relationship with one spouse, in Christ, for fruitfulness and holiness, and together living outwardly focused for the good of others. *Celibate* means unmarried, not drawn to marriage or even to dating, and experiencing spiritual fruitfulness through unusual availability to God's purposes. Celibacy does not automatically imply priesthood or religious life, or even living in community. Nor does celibacy imply a life of service within the church. It simply refers to a particular way of being in relationship with God and therefore with others.

We will explore these three vocational lifestyles—single, married, and celibate—in greater depth later in the chapter. But first, what do we mean by the term "vocational lifestyle"?

Vocational Lifestyle

We can easily think of lifestyle as something one chooses or pursues or fashions for oneself, such as "the lifestyles of the rich and famous," or the lifestyle of the artist, the bohemian lifestyle, the countercultural lifestyle, or any way of expressing yourself that both sets you apart from the social norm and

---

[41] I am indebted to Nemeck and Coombs for their writing on the three Christian lifestyles. See their *Called by God.*

aligns you with a particular group. But in terms of the Christian life, "lifestyle" means the *relational* way of life that best expresses who you are becoming in Christ and that most enables you to respond with all your heart, all your soul, all your mind, and all your strength to the circumstances of your life and times for the good of others. Christian vocational lifestyle is not a matter of choice, coincidence, luck, or default. Nor is Christian vocational lifestyle subject to the chance of meeting the right person, nor is it the curse of being the one left over.

Spiritually, your vocational lifestyle expresses God's relationship with you and your relationship with God, that core or generative relationship which gives shape and context and meaning to all your other relationships. In practical terms your vocational lifestyle supports both your work and your ways of engagement with the world. But oftentimes the connections here are neither automatic nor obvious. Many Christian men and women who are single or celibate may be living one or the other of these lifestyles long before they are able to identify or give words to the vocational dimensions of this experience. Even many who intentionally enter into Christian married life may not awaken immediately to the deeper vocational reality of the Christian lifestyle they have consciously and willingly embraced. God's calling is multilayered, finely nuanced, and endlessly evocative of one's deepest self over the course of a lifetime.

God, who is utter Simplicity, has no interest in confusing us as we figure out our vocational journey. So the dynamics of vocational lifestyle are not complex.

First, by virtue of your being human, and even more so by virtue of your baptism, you are *from* God, you are *for* God, and you are *returning to* God, through Christ who "holds all things together in himself."[42] You are anointed in Christ Jesus to participate in his redemptive work in the particular portion of the world which you have been given to inhabit and touch.

Second, *how* you live your anointing in this world is expressed specifically through your life which you live as single, married, or celibate. These lifestyles are not arbitrary or disconnected from your actual engagement in your world. You encounter the world through the prism of your relational commitments. Your vocational state in life facilitates the work which you are called upon and gifted to do. This God-centered way of living may well be counterintuitive to the way many people in our culture order their lives and prioritize their commitments. When "what I do" defines or even preempts "who I am" in relation to self, God, and others, I can count on eventual interior and relational collapse. We see this interior or existential collapse all too often, sadly and sometimes even tragically. Life lived away from the living center of all things soon becomes no life at all. For the baptized man or woman, the dynamic and ongoing conversation of self with the interior self, of self with God, and of self with others must precede, contextualize, animate, and sustain the work one does in this world.

To get a better understanding of life lived at the living center of all things—life lived in God, let's take a closer look at each of the three vocational lifestyles, beginning with singlehood, and examine how they work.

---

[42] See Colossians 1:17.

We All Start Out Single

In my senior year in an all-girls Catholic high school, I remember a classmate, Annie, asking a question in religion class. "If sex is for marriage, then why did God give single people all this equipment?" For a moment we all sat in stunned silence. Although I was still painfully shy around boys, I had a hunch that many of my classmates were not. All eyes were poised on Sister, whom we all presumed could not possess a meaningful vocabulary on the topic of sex.

Still, a good number of us were silently grateful for Annie's question, and hopeful of an answer that would make sense and shed light on our young and awakening lives.

The truth is, we all start out single. And as long as we live, our lives are a work in progress. Singlehood, which vocationally often is a transitional lifestyle, is best understood in the context of Christian marriage or celibate life.

The young adult years are the time we are given to explore how God is calling us relationally. This is a time when friendships begin to be formed independent of family ties. Knowing and being known by others—especially by those who enter our world apart from the family circle—evokes in us a new sense of personhood. Some young people "just know" at a deep level that God is preparing them for Christian marriage. Dating for them is not idle entertainment but a process of discerning what God might have in mind.

Some young adults may remain single into their thirties, and even into their middle years, holding in their heart a calling to Christian married life. Yet oftentimes they have a hunch that where they are in their life right now— perhaps committed to caring for aging parents, or involved in studies or in work that is meaningful and fulfilling but that requires long stretches of travel—is where God seems pleased to meet them at this time. While they carry the dream and openness to marriage, they also experience the peace of being fully present to their current life circumstances.

In the course of spiritual direction some directees do not consider their state in life as needing any exploration. Perhaps they assume that their vocational state in life has no real bearing on the conversation. Yet when a person becomes "single again" following a marriage relationship, a telltale restlessness may pervade the conversation, indicating that something needs to be addressed. Oftentimes in situations of divorce or loss of spouse through death, the directee's focus may turn to addressing the trauma and the deep waves of grief.

Active processing of such loss and trauma deserves unrushed and graced reflection, both alone and with a trusted spiritual guide. Only when the time is right can conversation turn to the vocational lifestyle to which God may be calling the newly single person. The spiritual work here is not to assume that the directee will set out to find another spouse, or just remain "unmarried." Rather, the spiritual work is to explore what God has in mind for this particular person at this particular juncture in life, and to begin to move toward openness to God's willing. Wise vocational direction can bring clarity, interior peace, a renewed sense of purpose, and a gentle new movement of one's life in God's direction.

Many, but not all, who become divorced or widowed return to the single state—meaning, many, but not all, become open again to the possibility of marriage.[43] Some may enter into an active celibate state, as we shall see below. Once you have passed through grief to a "holy recentering" in your life, a new discernment of vocational lifestyle can begin. Singlehood, or openness to the possibility of dating and marriage, is always both a state in life and a state of grace when it gives expression to God's willing. And because it usually is a

---

[43] A caution here: Multiple marriages that end in divorce can often indicate that the person never was called by God to Christian married life but possibly to Christian celibate life. Repeated failures at marriage send a loud and clear signal that a fundamental shift is needed: from *deciding* who to marry next to *discerning* God's wise and perfect plan for the individual's happiness. Premarriage pastoral sessions must fearlessly and candidly address this discernment in a more focused way, first of all by dropping the assumption that the two people seeking to be married have already discerned an authentic call by God to enter into Christian married life and to marry each other.

transitional vocational lifestyle, singlehood matures into a clear calling once again to Christian married life, or, in some instances, to celibate life, either in the lay state or as a consecrated religious.

Christian Marriage: The Social and Vocational Norm

Reflecting back on my high school classmate Annie's question about marriage, the "equipment" of sexual union matters in the human conjugal expression, within marriage, of the spiritually intimate and self-giving union with God within the human soul. Marriage is defended socially as the normal and necessary context for bringing forth and raising children and bringing a foundational social order that fosters stability within society. Even more, Christian marriage is esteemed by the church as a means of grace and the path to holiness for the married couple.

Vocationally, Christian marriage offers a living witness to the power of relationship that exists for the sake of the other. Christian marriage is infused with the movement of the Holy Spirit, moving the couple in their sublime, their mundane, and their challenging moments in God's direction of mutual self-giving salvific love.

Oftentimes in my spiritual direction practice, I have found that if I did not overtly ask the question "Are you married?" the directee and I could go several sessions before this vocationally vital piece of information is revealed. Your vocational state in life is a core element of your personhood, shaping the ways you are the presence of Christ in the world. It deserves a place in the holy conversation between director and directee. Why?

As the *Catechism of the Catholic Church* states, Christian marriage is "a bond ... which ... is perpetual and exclusive," in which the spouses are "strengthened and ... consecrated for the duties and the dignity of their state."[44] John Paul II spoke often of marriage as it was meant to be before the Fall, a

---

[44] See *CCC,* para. 1638.

relationship not of domination and submission but of mutual self-giving.[45] Christian marriage points the spouses toward Christ, who is the dynamic and unitive force of married love.

With Christ as the center, the couple matures in understanding their unique vocational mission in the world. Their "perpetual and exclusive" union brings not only order and stability to home and society; it brings Christ himself. How this vision of Christian marriage is revealed—or not—within the directee's experience is worthy of reflection in spiritual direction.

Signs for Discerning Marriage

"Choosing" the vocational lifestyle of Christian marriage does not mean that this lifestyle has chosen you. In fact, *choosing* any of the vocational lifestyles—especially married life or celibate life—is spiritually dangerous work. In *Discerning Vocations to Marriage, Celibacy and Singlehood*, authors Nemeck and Coombs offer a series of necessary signs and conditions for discerning an authentic calling to Christian married life.[46] My informal survey of men and women who have cycled through Christian marriage, sometimes multiple times, reveals that these considerations were not part of the discernment conversation prior to their marriage.

Important considerations, according to Nemeck and Coombs, in discerning God's calling and the readiness of the couple to enter into Christian marriage and to marry each other include questions concerning:

- sufficient emotional, psychological, affective, and sexual maturity;
- adequate self-understanding, knowledge of the other, and sense of self-identity; and

---

[45] See, for example, Christopher West, *Theology of the Body for Beginners: A Basic Introduction to Pope John Paul II's Sexual Revolution* (West Chester, PA: Ascension, 2004).

[46] See Nemeck and Coombs, *Discerning Vocations,* chapters 5 to 11 on Married Life, esp. 98–99, on signs and conditions of readiness for marriage.

- adequate interdependence balanced with a respect for their own and the other's solitude and privacy.

Other important considerations include:

- shared religious convictions and spiritual interests;
- the ability to share wedded life in peace and harmony; and
- a mature love that supports a lifelong conjugal covenant.

Finally, and most compellingly, the discernment of readiness for the two to enter into Christian married life addresses the couple's existential inability to *not* marry each other in their journey into fullness of personhood-in-God.

Ultimately, this thorough discernment of God's calling to Christian married life is the two individuals' expression of faith, of a dynamic and radical trust—in God and in each other. With marriage upheld as the norm in society and in the church, young people oftentimes feel social or family pressure to enter into marriage when their true calling is to celibate life, or to married life but not with this person, or to married life with this person but after either or both of them have undergone a necessary maturing.

Trying to honor a well-intentioned but mistaken marriage is a sure path to spiritual anguish. The rigors of a deep and unrushed discernment cannot be dismissed simply because these two people are "so obviously in love." Our hurry-up culture, the subtleties of peer pressure, the glamour and sizzle of the multibillion dollar bridal industry, family expectations, financial practicalities, the need to drive out loneliness—these forces as well as others obstruct a clear and honest discernment of a call to Christian married life.

Expressions of Christian Married Life

What might a vocationally alive Christian marriage look like as it is lived day to day? Couples I know readily come to mind for their generosity of home and heart, their care for the needs of others, their outward reach to share their time and their talents.

I experience the power of Christian marriage in my friends Kathy and Steve. With no children of their own, they prayed for God's guidance in the life of their then childless marriage. Over the years they have adopted four children. Their married life and Christ-centered home is the milieu in which God's healing love can penetrate deeply into young and complex lives.

My friend Catherine, now ninety, recalls how, on her wedding day, her husband Don said, "Honey, we will commit our household to tithing." She did not realize that he meant tithing fifty percent of his (their only) income. By the time their fourth child arrived, Catherine was adept at stretching Don's fifty-percent paycheck to the end of the month. When a co-worker asked Don if he knew of a doctor who could perform an abortion, Don pledged to pay every medical bill through the remaining months of the co-worker's wife's pregnancy and delivery, and equally covered all expenses for the newborn's adoption.

Benedict and Ellen, a Catholic married couple and university professors, spend four weeks each year in a small parish in Santiago, Chile, forming catechists who are learning to confidently and competently form families in Christian faith within their cluster of parishes. Benedict and Ellen met over thirty years ago as participants in a group dedicated to the social justice teachings of the Gospel, and sharing their Christian faith and vibrant missionary zeal. That shared passion for the Gospel and for God's people has served as the source of ongoing spiritual rejuvenation within their marriage.

It's easy to think, "Well, those are the heroic examples of married life." But in my spiritual direction practice I hear story after story of how God works in powerful ways not only within marriages but through marriages, accomplishing amazing things because this particular marriage relationship exists with Christ as the center. One after another, many married directees have affirmed their deep-seated conviction that God has called them to Christian married life—with this particular person. And one after another, many married directees radiate a deep knowing that they are vocationally alive, and that through their marriage they are living out their vocational purpose. In some instances directees have finally found words, in the direction setting, to express the vocational reality—and vocational joy—of their Christian married life.

A Fresh Look at Celibate Life

A lot of misperception surrounds Christian celibate life—a way of life which is not socially the norm within the pattern of human relationship, nor is it the norm even among those who are baptized. Yet for some men and women it is an anointed way of life that brings spiritual vitality to the church and to the world. How shall we describe Christian celibate life?

Simply, the celibate man or woman lives an unmarried yet spiritually fruitful life which enables that person to be unusually available to God's purposes in the church or in the world. Currently the norm in the Roman Catholic Church is for celibate male clergy and celibate male and female consecrated religious. But even here we find variance emerging, with married male clergy from Protestant churches entering the Roman rite and becoming active priests. And with the rise of "new monasticism" we find intentional contemplative and apostolic communities, living peaceably, prayerfully, and productively under the guidance of a written Rule and the blessing of the bishop. Typically these communities welcome men and women across all three vocational states—celibate, single, and married.

An important distinction exists between the terms "celibate at heart"—referring to an individual's actual charism for celibate life, and "celibate by circumstance"—meaning living unmarried in order to fulfill a requirement for ministry or mission, or, in the case of divorce or widowhood, living unmarried as a result of the loss of a spouse but lacking a clear sense of calling to remarriage. A person who is "celibate by circumstance" in order to fulfill, say, requirements for ministry, may in fact be vocationally single and ultimately called by God to Christian married life. Spiritual fruitfulness for a person in this situation will be tempered by the angst of such an interior sacrifice.

Celibacy as a vocational lifestyle is a *positive* calling to fullness of personhood in this particular manner. The willing Christian celibate man or woman experiences a particular direction and purpose that flows from a spiritually intimate relationship with the Lord and an unusual availability to God's purposes, which may involve ministry within the church, or mission through wholehearted engagement in the world.

Celibacy as Vocational Imperative

For those called by God to celibate life, this way of life becomes a dynamic vocational imperative. These individuals often find that they experience a quiet joy, an inner centeredness in Christ; and over time they feel a complete inability to even imagine leaving this way of life for married life. In fact, dating, for them, would be a frustrating interruption.

I have encountered Christian celibate men and women in law, medicine, social services, advocacy, public service, the sciences, the arts, education—all demanding professions—who find that in their lives they simply have no time or interior inclination to dedicate themselves to the rightful demands and commitments of married life. Their lives as celibate men and women of faith are also unusually fruitful and effective; they feel fulfilled in the apostolic dimensions of their work, a convincing indicator that their work is not an escape from the demands of relationship nor a way to fill a relational void in their life. Rather, they experience their lives as a way of serving God and others and thus revealing the reign of God.

One reason lay celibates seldom talk about their calling is that oftentimes they have no vocabulary to speak meaningfully about their experience. For many, they have grown into Christian celibate life seemingly by default. And for some, being described as celibate when they sense no clear calling to priesthood or consecrated religious life can feel like a respectable term for "loner." Most people within the church have never heard a clear distinction between singlehood and celibacy as vocational lifestyles. To frustrate the vocational lifestyle discernment even more, online matchmaking services—yes, even Christian-oriented matchmaking services—create static in the delicate work of discerning God's particular willing for your life.[47]

Bringing discernment of the celibate vocational state in life to the light of spiritual direction can help a directee to recognize already existing patterns of spiritual fruitfulness in a way of life they may have been unable to name or wholeheartedly embrace. Such conversation can bring clarity and joy to the directee's pursuit of God's purposes.

Discerning Celibate Life

I was 52 before I could name God's calling of me to celibate life. When I finally put the clues together, my lifelong pattern of "not being married" suddenly made sense. All through my young adult years and straight through my forties I could never really picture myself as married, and I intuitively sensed that if I were to become married, the marriage would not last. At age 50 I was willing to consider a celibate marriage—not because I was afraid of the many dimensions of intimacy that define a marriage relationship but because I had in mind a man who probably was as called to celibate life as I was. When no relationship developed, I finally gave God permission to capture my attention and claim my freedom. With this bold step I felt liberated to live *for God*

[47] Online dating has complexified discernment of vocational lifestyle, especially for newly single adults. Finding that one particular man or woman who is just right—and a person of Christian faith, too!—does not mean that God has intended you at this time to enter into Christian married life, and with this particular person. The ease of a mouse click can frustrate the delicate and spiritually fine-tuned discernment process. People who have gone through divorce, especially multiple times, may experience the impossibility of fruitfully pursuing the vocational lifestyle of Christian marriage when the grace clearly waits elsewhere. The social, familial, and economic pressures to pursue marriage further complicate the discernment process.

wholeheartedly; I experienced for the first time living a life which felt as though it actually had my name on it.[48]

So how *do* you discern a calling to celibate life? For lay celibates in the church, there is no sacrament or ritual or defining moment when one "becomes celibate." For those discerning God's calling to marriage, or to celibate priesthood or traditional consecrated religious life, clarity regarding the celibate vocational lifestyle is imperative before one enters into the vows or promises of the particular vocational state. The person genuinely called and gifted by God to celibate life is not "giving up sex" or the prospects of family life. They are not really "giving up" anything. If you feel that you are placing on the altar of sacrifice some core relational dimension of your being, this may be your first clue that you are pushing away from the way of life in which God desires you to be most generously and fruitfully your authentic self. An abiding sense of joy is the hallmark of God's calling. Celibate men and women experience a *positive freedom* to be most fully their authentic self-in-God, unmarried, in fruitful service in the church or in the world.

How can the spiritual direction conversation guide the discernment of a possible calling to celibate life? First, it is essential that the director have the vocational vocabulary to hear and interpret accurately both what *is* being said and what is *not* being said, and to speak confidently and gently so that a helpful discernment can occur.

Second, as a directee, look together with the director for patterns of fruitfulness already evident in your life; look for the recurring interests, inclinations, and preferred ways of living. Perhaps you experience a take-it-or-leave-it attitude about dating, or seem unable to really picture yourself in a lifelong marriage relationship. Hopefulness for marriage may keep cropping up, but it may keep dissolving in disappointment. Especially if there is always some

---

[48] An in-depth discussion of discernment of the celibate Christian lifestyle is presented in my audio CD *Christian Celibate Life: Discerning the Authentic Gift* (Eugene, OR: Awakening Vocations, 2011) (www.awakeningvocations.com).

reason for the disappointment or lost opportunity, look for the pattern, acknowledge it, and recognize that even your most ardent prayer for "someone to love" is perhaps being answered in a way you had not imagined.

Do look for recurring patterns of joy or quiet satisfaction already present in your life. You may find deep enjoyment in giving your time and energies to causes you care about, or to caring for loved ones or others who benefit from your presence—time which otherwise would be given to spouse, family, and home life. Celibate people oftentimes feel most fulfilled when they are deeply engaged in the interface between contemplative prayer and apostolic works.

If you are wondering if God has chosen you for celibate life, ask yourself these questions:

1. Do I enjoy a rich and deeply sustaining friendship with the Lord which gives life to all other relationships?
2. Do I find a pattern of resisting the "intrusion" of dating or resisting others' encouragement to pursue marriage?
3. Do I experience unusual joy in being available to God's purposes?

None of these questions alone can confirm a celibate lifestyle, but all are worthy of the holy conversation of spiritual and vocational direction. These questions, combined with prayerful reflection on your experience and life circumstances, can serve to guide your discernment of vocational lifestyle.

Lay celibates, by and large, are an unrecognized and certainly untapped treasure in the church's mission in the world of the twenty-first century. This lay vocational state in life goes ritually uncelebrated and therefore largely undefined, overlooked, and undiscerned. The Christian community for the most part lacks a vocabulary to speak of the validity, the urgency, and the power of the celibate vocational lifestyle. A lot of potential, sadly, goes to waste, and many "undiscerned single" men and women just drift away from what they experience as the family-centered parish.

Cautions in Premature Discernment of Vocational Lifestyle

I remember when "no-fault divorce" came into the headlines. How sensible! And then came the trendy and practical prenuptial agreement. How prudent! Lifetime commitments never were very realistic, so the logic goes, given the great obstacle they can pose to personal freedom.

But we would be wise to slow down and take a deeper look. For God's anointed ones, life can never honestly be about "me and mine." Unrushed and theologically sound vocational discernment must be the norm for *every* baptized man, woman, young adult, and youth, especially when lifelong solemn commitments are at stake. As members of a church with a divine mission and mandate, we must insist that such vocational discernment be the norm. Especially because the church receives the solemn vows of those who enter into certain lifelong vocational commitments, the church owes those entering into such commitments access to a thorough and honest discernment to prevent premature choices that can lead to everything from personal anguish and relentless heartache to destructive attitudes and behaviors and the irreparable distortion of one's personhood.

Where do we usually go wrong in our process of discerning vocational lifestyle? Even in the church of the twenty-first century we continue to struggle with the following:

- A narrow understanding of "vocation," which is in fact a Gospel value which applies to *every baptized person in every stage of life;*
- Lack of a robust theology of vocation springing from Baptism and Confirmation, understandable enough to shape and impel every baptized man, woman, young adult, and youth to take personal responsibility for the church's mission in the world;
- The tendency to confuse "decision making" with an actual discernment process—a process which requires humility, trust, mature guidance,

honest listening, reflection on one's life and circumstances, and openness to God's willing and the movement of the Holy Spirit.

A wholehearted response to God's calling presumes a wholehearted relationship with God, with Jesus, with the Holy Spirit, and with the church. This wholehearted response also presumes the availability of, and openness to, vocational guidance at the personal as well as the parish level, vocational guidance that is readily and easily accessible and understandable to every person through every stage of life.[49]

---

[49] My "Vocational Guide Formation" workshop, part of the Awakening Vocations suite of workshops, forms parish-based vocational guides to fulfill this discernment imperative. See www.awakeningvocations.com/parishresources.

Bringing It Home

1. Given the vocational definitions of single, married, and celibate life, what evidence can I point to in my life that suggests that I am actually living the vocational lifestyle to which I have been called by God?

2. What (or who) has been most helpful in my process of discerning my vocational lifestyle? What specific story can I share?

3. What might I be accomplishing within the reign of God—in the church or in my world—that I perhaps could not accomplish, or not accomplish as well, if I were living a different vocational lifestyle?

Hold this Thought

The vocational lifestyle which God has in mind for me

is a path to my greatest happiness.

7

YOU STAND ANOINTED

Confirmation as Expression of Spiritual Maturity

In eighth grade I remember the catechism drills we went through to prepare for Confirmation. The deeper we went into that little pale blue covered book, the less certain I felt about my ability to memorize.

Secretly, I had my worries. Will the bishop hurl a question at me? If he does, will I remember the answer? I should, because I think of myself as a better than average student and I am paying *very careful attention* as we go page by page through the questions. If the bishop calls on me, will I be able to recall the answer quickly, and then speak it out correctly? Will I stumble with my words? Will my peers laugh? (Probably not, because they know they could be next.) Will I shame my parents? Will I come away with an indelible emotional scar?

What are the odds the bishop will even call my name? And when he slaps my face with the back of his hand. This all feels so … *intimidating*.

Ruminating over these things for weeks on end, my stomach

churned.

I am happy to report that the bishop did not call on me, but the slap to the face bore a startling and curious sting—perhaps because it was "nothing personal."

Maybe that approach to "Confirmation prep" was more the bishop's test of Sister's ability to teach than it was about my readiness to own my Christian faith in a living way. But that was then, and this is now— the only point in time for which I am accountable in the present tense.

In fact, each one of us is accountable in the present tense for the living faith with which we have been entrusted. And while we may not think of our day-to-day lives in these terms, the language of living faith is the language best cultivated in the holy conversation of spiritual and vocational direction.

More than a One-time Event

We can easily think of Confirmation—and any of the church's sacraments—as one-time events.[50] In a way, they are. You prepare, you rehearse, you dress up for the occasion and go through it, and then it's done. Yet the power and purpose of each sacrament unfolds over time. How so with Confirmation?

Confirmation is situated among the church's sacraments of initiation which orient you interiorly, by the deep working of the Holy Spirit, toward God's perfect willing. This sacrament is not only for your own spiritual good but for the spiritual good of those whose lives you will touch over the course of your lifetime—and they will be many.

So the anointing, or *chrismation,* with perfumed oil which you received

---

[50] Many of the ideas in this chapter are more fully examined in my book, *Anointed for a Purpose: Confirmed for Life in the Twenty-first Century* (Eugene, OR: Awakening Vocations, 2012).

in Confirmation is an initiating event in your lifelong process of what we might call "christification"[51] or participation in divine life. St. Paul describes this work of christification as your becoming subject to Christ as Christ is subject to the Father, "so that God may be all in all."[52] Your christification empowers you not only to move in God's direction but to move into God. This sacramental process of God's life at work within you, and therefore your divinization, begins with Baptism. God's life at work within you is affirmed, confirmed, and made strong in this sacrament we call Confirmation.[53] As you mature, this anointing unfolds and bears fruit in ways you might not have imagined, especially as you become increasingly responsible for your relationship with the risen Lord and with his holy Spirit.

All of this maturing—or sometimes resistance to maturing—becomes worthy matter for conversation in spiritual and vocational direction. Why? Because at the heart of Christian faith lies not a logic but a scandal—the scandal of God's generosity in the work of redemption. Every one of us should be somewhat baffled and confused by the enormity of the offer God holds out to us —to participate in the life and intimate communion of love which is the very essence of the Holy Trinity. These are the deeper things, the deeper truths, the deeper realities that shape and continually strive to shape us at every turn. The scandal of God's generosity at work in our lives becomes increasingly the focus of spiritual growth in the ever-maturing directee's life.

Consider in what ways, and to what extent, these three aspects of Confirmation resonate in your life now:

1. Confirmation means *being confirmed*, or *standing strong*, in God's intention for your life—within the Christian community and for the

---

[51] See Nemeck and Coombs, *The Way of Spiritual Direction*, chap. 1, esp. 15, 20–23.

[52] See 1 Corinthians 15:28.

[53] See *CCC*, para. 1289.

sake of the world, according to your state in life and the ways you have been gifted.

2. Confirmation is *your statement within the Christian community* of standing firm with God among the ranks of the faithful, anointed in the power of the Holy Spirit to be the living presence of the risen Lord for the world you now touch.

3. Confirmation, ultimately, is *God's Yes* to you, to your life, your purpose, and your destiny; it is also *your Yes* to your life, purpose, and destiny, even though you cannot fully understand, or even imagine, what this means at this time.

Being anointed in the Holy Spirit confirms that you have spiritually meaningful and important work to do in this world in the course of your life. Confirmation is the church's powerful affirmation of the dignity and responsibility of your profession of faith in the risen Lord and your share in his Spirit. Confirmation is also the church's public and sacramental affirmation of your share in the work of revealing the reign of God in your time. In this sense, Confirmation can be called not only a sacrament of initiation but a sacrament of vocation—a lifelong expression of God's calling and your response.

Lifelong Relationship: God Calls, You Respond

There is nothing magical or automatic about your anointing in Confirmation, no plug-and-play features that let you sit back and enjoy the ride. Like all the other sacraments, Confirmation is first and foremost a dynamic and lifelong *expression of relationship*—first, your relationship with the risen Lord, and therefore with the Christian community, and the moving outward, an intentional expression of your relationship with the people and circumstances, the institutions and initiatives that you will encounter in the course of your life.

The effects of your anointing in Confirmation unfold over the span of your life as you mature into your relationship with Jesus and his mission, a relationship nourished most deeply within the Christian community. The dynamics of this lifelong relationship are straightforward: God calls, you respond. God initiates everything. You may get plenty of ideas and take plenty of action over the course of your life, but it is always, *always* God who initiates, and you, in turn, who respond. Spiritual and vocational direction offers you the opportunity to examine how this dynamic of God's calling and your response is at work in your life, and examine, too, the ways in which it might be fettered or side-tracked.

This lifelong relationship with God, animated and guided by the Holy Spirit, is the *vocational* dimension of Confirmation. God's calling is embedded in relationship, and your response depends on the *quality* of your relationship with God, and therefore the quality of your relationship with self and with others. For the relationship to be authentic, you need to actually be present—not present and distracted, but present and wholeheartedly engaged. Apart from such engagement, you have no way of living the life which is authentically yours. Responding to God's calling requires a disciplined interior life, but Jesus reminds us that it is a yoke that fits easily upon the shoulders, so that the best of your strength can go to the task.[54]

While God's actual calling—perhaps different from what you had pictured—may feel like an interruption, it actually is perfectly of a piece with the trajectory of your anointed life according to God's desiring. God's calling will always ask of you all your heart, all your soul, all your mind, and all your strength in a way that engages what is most worthy and gifted and vital within you. God's calling is so perfectly suited to *you* that you realize one day that you cannot imagine *not* living this particular life, with these particular people, and doing this work that engages you in heart, soul, mind, and strength, at this particular time.

But before God calls you to *do something,* God calls you to *be someone:* to be the self whom God has desired eternally. Being any less than this requires a lot more energy to sustain, because here you are working *against* your

---

[54] See Matthew 11:28–30, esp. v. 30.

God-given authentic nature, which is to be whole and holy in God. In Baptism and Confirmation you have been anointed for so much more than the low threshold of engagement which seems to define so much of life in our culture today.

Anointed for a Purpose

Taking the long view, the most recent historic step forward in the life of the church came in the course of the Second Vatican Council, when the church awakened with new vigor to its mission: *to exist for the sake of the world.* The landmark document, *The Pastoral Constitution on the Church in the Modern World,*[55] was startling in its insistence that the church's mission is to engage in real dialogue with contemporary society, exist for the good of the world and its salvation, and actively address the world's concerns through the lens of the Gospel. This awakening has led the church to reposition for the real business of working, teaching, and advocating at all levels of society for life, justice, mercy, and peacemaking—all vital expressions of the reign of God.

With this awakening and repositioning within the church now commenced, what comes next? The next historic step forward in the life of the church will come when you and I finally awaken to our real capacity to take Pentecost seriously and to carry the fire outward. The risen Lord breathed his Spirit into the Apostles,[56] and from that moment on their lives—and our world— were set on a new trajectory. We live today, amazingly, with this same Spirit, confirmed in the same mission of revealing the risen Lord in a complex, sometimes hostile, and sometimes indifferent world.

The Scriptures have given us another image of Pentecost, too, of

---

[55] *Pastoral Constitution on the Church in the Modern World,* in *Vatican Council II: Vol. 1: The Conciliar and Post Conciliar Documents,* Austin Flannery, OP, gen. ed. (Northport, NY: Costello, 1975, 1996), 903–1001.

[56] See John 20:21–22.

tongues of fire that came to rest on each of the Apostles.[57] Each received a very personal empowerment in the Holy Spirit—not so that the Apostles could "be like" Jesus, but so that they could actually stand with full authority in his place and confidently do his works.

In our post-Vatican II twenty-first century it is still easy to think that being *like* Jesus is enough. But being like Jesus misses the point. We are not anointed to "be like" Jesus, one step removed from the Real Presence. We are anointed to *be* that Real Presence in sometimes hidden but always gifted ways. We carry his breath within us. The Holy Spirit empowers us—each and together —to stand with authority, humility, and faith in the place of Jesus to reveal the reign of God in our own unique time and place. To stand in such radical trust is a gift of the Holy Spirit and a sure confirmation of our anointing.

A steadfast radical trust in God sets you free, over time, to live a bold and generous life for God and to stand wholeheartedly in the place of Jesus. Your standing firm in radical trust gives the Holy Spirit capacity to accomplish through you "greater things than these."[58]

While it is easy to focus on immediate personal concerns in spiritual direction, you in fact have a much bigger and much bolder work to consider, a work that requires a clarity of purpose and passion beyond what you alone can imagine. How you live the challenge of Pentecost over the course of your life is worthy and important material for the holy conversation of spiritual and vocational direction.

Confirmed, Conformed, and Not Alone

The sacrament of Confirmation can also be described as the sacrament of "conformation," of your being "conformed to Christ." In Confirmation you

---

[57] See Acts 2:1–4.

[58] See John 14:12.

have entered a stage in life where you now become increasingly personally responsible for carrying Jesus' love, healing, and redemption to the world. You have been anointed into an amazing and dynamic partnership, and the partnership has now begun. You now move from being a follower or disciple of Jesus to being one who is anointed in the Spirit of the risen Lord and sent for a purpose. Your life as a true apostle begins to take a more recognizable shape. Willingly and over time you enter more deeply into the work of your christification—your "becoming" in Christ. Surely it is a unique and solitary journey, yet not one that is isolated from the Christian community. In your anointing you begin your necessary journey into the mystery of God. If this sounds like the language of paschal mystery, it is: dying to self in order to rise to new life in the living Christ.

In the context of spiritual and vocational direction, this awakening to your real work of christification oftentimes is expressed in life circumstances that do not make sense, in the things that should not be happening to you, the things that do not fit the script as you have imagined it. Being conformed to Christ means experiencing your life and *your* direction of your life being taken from you, *your* power and effectiveness being taken from you, until you reach the point where all you can do is surrender to the unseen and perhaps quite distant-feeling providence of God. If we understand the writings of St. Paul correctly, every person, every living being, undergoes this work of christification.[59] The wise spiritual director does not turn from this painful work which overtakes you but remains present, the attentive midwife as you undergo this excruciating and humbling birthing into your greater self-in-God. It is imperative that the spiritual director has already undergone in some measure this deep, anguished, and purifying work of christification, because the urge to gloss over it will be strong.

The Christian community, too, must be a source of encouragement and strength in this intense work of your christification. Every one of us needs regular engagement in the deep nourishing of the table of Word and Eucharist,

---

[59] See, for example, 1 Corinthians 15:28, Ephesians 4:6, Colossians 3:11.

and to experience the goodness of being in company—*in communion*—with all fellow believers who are undergoing, or who have undergone, or who soon enough will undergo, this deep work of christification.

The point of this painful and intensely personal work of being conformed to Christ is not to initiate you into a lifetime of suffering but rather, to initiate you into the lifelong work of standing in the place of Christ. By your anointing in the Holy Spirit you discover the authority and the dignity of this anointing, and the fellowship of communion of all the holy ones, both those who are living and those who have gone before you and opened the way.

Career or Calling

This lifelong unfolding and animation of the sacrament of Confirmation has vocational implications, which play out in the work you do and the career or calling which you pursue. But vocationally, career and calling can be two very different things, yielding over the span of a lifetime two very different outcomes. Let's take a closer look at these two words.

Career comes from the word for road or racecourse, meaning: "to get on the course that gets you somewhere." It refers to the path or the route one takes to reach a fixed destination. Career carries with it a sense of certainty, both in the desired destination and the best path to reach it. Interestingly, the word *career* is uncomfortably close to the word *careen,* which means to lean from side to side, or to lurch unpredictably. There is something "ungraceful" about this careening, especially as it might describe one's career.

In a vocational sense, *calling* is very different from this popular notion of career. Calling is not about you choosing a sure path toward an appealing destination, but about God desiring the full glory of your personhood and communicating that desire to you in the circumstances of your life; and in response, you embrace what God's eternal desiring already has set in motion.

The difference between career and calling is the difference between "success" (often measured in financial or material terms) and "fruitfulness," a spiritual quality which comes forth when you are alive in God. Over time, and with grace, many people wake up to the truth that they would rather trust God than trust their own ability to set the best route for their lives. But trusting God means that you actually let go your urge to control. In a sense you exit the driver's seat and hand over the car keys. In fact, you trust God *because* holding on to the car keys and mapping out your own itinerary no longer makes sense.

The Gospels offer vocational insight and encouragement as we discern our way through the career-or-calling maze. Jesus taught his followers, "So do not worry and say, 'What are we to eat?' or 'What are we … to wear?' … Your heavenly Father knows [what] you need. … But seek first the kingdom [of God] and his righteousness, and all these things will be given you besides" (Matthew 6:31–33). These were not the poetic notions of some dreamy-eyed romantic. Jesus was speaking a core spiritual truth.

"But seek first the kingdom of God" is a profoundly vocational phrase with deep theological implications. When what you do is an expression of God's perfect plan for your life, you *are* living your vocation. And when what you do is out of step with God's perfect plan, you will find over time that relationship with God careens, lurches unpredictably, slips out of focus, falls off center.

How will you know that your work life is grounded in God's perfect plan? First, your prayer and your work will be in harmony; your work will flow from your relationship with God through prayer. You will discover an ease and grace in what you do. You will feel energized, and your work will be unusually effective. You will become like the person who finds a treasure hidden in a field, and who quickly goes and sells everything in order to buy that field, or like the merchant in search of fine pearls who finds one pearl of great value and sells everything in order to buy it.[60]

---

[60] See Matthew 13:44–46.

Living Your Vocation

How do you get to the point of actually living your vocation? In part you will find your way because the Holy Spirit ultimately will not let you fail. This does not mean that you will be spared the anguish and setbacks of poorly chosen actions or the injustices of others' greed or negligence. But also in part the wise counsel of a truly gifted director will enable you to see the things that God would have you see, and will give you encouragement to act accordingly.

Here is a five-step process to discern where you are with God's calling, a process which you may find helpful to repeat throughout the course of your life.

First, *let go* your tightly held plans and your understanding of the way things should be, and *prayerfully open yourself* to God's perfect plan, God's perfect desiring for your life, and God's perfect timing.

Second, *notice* things. Notice what in the world is going on; notice what in *your* world is going on. Notice what is occurring or shifting. Notice where the needs are and how you feel empowered or gifted or qualified to respond. Notice in your work any patterns of effectiveness—or ineffectiveness. Notice what might be emerging on your vocational horizon.

Third, *take action.* Engage the Holy Spirit; work *with* the Holy Spirit. Enter into the living, dynamic partnership which the Holy Spirit already has offered you. Step forward; give it a try.

Fourth, *prayerfully examine your results.* Take time regularly—weekly if not daily—to reflect on how the Spirit of the risen Lord is alive in you, guiding your actions, opening your insight, bringing you to a clearer understanding, abiding with you in your times of not understanding, and moving you ever more surely in God's direction.

Fifth, *take the next courageous step.* This may mean making a phone call, initiating that difficult conversation; taking care of tasks you have been putting off, catching up on reading, visiting a friend. God can work with any of that and all of that. But give God something to work with.

Living out God's calling in your life is not just about choosing the right field of study or pursuing the right profession—or even taking the right job. You will never know the mind of God, nor will you ever achieve real and permanent vocational certainty. Yet you can rest in knowing that God is too deeply invested in you to let you ultimately fail. Your primary vocational concern is to be your uniquely anointed self, God-directed, empowered by the Holy Spirit to live the life and to do the work which enables you to reveal the reign of God according to the ways you have been gifted.

Anointed for Peacemaking

When we consider Confirmation as a lifetime event we may not immediately think of peacemaking as an expression of this anointed way of life. We may think that peacemaking is not our immediate concern, that it is best left to someone else, someone who is skilled in diplomacy, perhaps, or someone who is willing to engage in the risky work of passive resistance. Peacemaking as an expression of Christian faith requires us to take our relationship with Jesus, the preeminently nonviolent One, to a more serious level. Jesus' injunction to his followers to be peacemakers raises the stakes for true disciples. The challenging work of becoming a peacemaker can raise the threshold of holiness well beyond our comfort zone.

Interestingly, "Blessed are the peacemakers" was not the first of the beatitudes which Jesus taught[61] but the seventh—not because peacemaking is less important than being poor in spirit, which is the first of the beatitudes. Rather, being poor in spirit, mourning what needs to be mourned, being meek and not pushy, hungering and thirsting for God's righteousness, and being merciful and pure of heart, all are *conversion points* on the way to peacemaking. Jesus considered peacemaking not one among many virtues, but the preeminent

---

[61] See Matthew 5:3–12.

expression of the reign of God, and which requires the wholehearted living of these other interior attitudes for its own vital expression.

As he hung in the slow anguished process of his execution, Jesus brought the divine kiss of peace to the criminal who acknowledged him as Messiah. And following his resurrection, Jesus' first words to the apostles were: "Peace be with you" (John 20:19, 22, 26). Of all the things he could have said as he walked through the locked doors of that upper room, these were his opening words, spoken three times, and captured by the Evangelist. No words mocking those who thought they had finally gotten rid of him; no words of gloating, no words, even, of looking back in any way. *Peace be with you,* the risen Lord said —words that continue to reveal the presence of the reign of God here and now. The Gospels point to *peace* as expressing the very essence of the reign of God, and peace which sets that reign of God in motion.

The church from the earliest days cherished and protected the preeminence of this gift of peace, and witnessed to the deeply conversional quality of the practice of peacemaking. In three Gospel accounts we hear Jesus' admonition to his followers to "put away the sword."[62] And in the unnerving witness of the early Christians before the lions (prompting the conversion of some of their persecutors), they stood steadfast in peace in the face of mad violence as their sign of faith in the Lord's nonviolent triumph over the forces of evil and death. Injustices and mad violence continue today, calling forth from a new generation of followers new expressions of forgiveness, reconciliation, and peacemaking.

How does the church's witness of peace personally concern you? Perhaps you just want to mind your own affairs, be kind, do no harm, and get along with people. But you are anointed in the Holy Spirit for something far greater than just getting along. Even if you just get along, minding your own affairs, a spiritual restlessness sooner or later will challenge you to speak up or

---

[62] See Matthew 26:52; Luke 22:51; John 18:11.

act in the cause of justice which is the foundation of peace.[63] That restlessness is the interior stirring of the Holy Spirit, and your invitation to deeper engagement.

Rejection of violence in all its active and passive forms, a firm commitment to peacemaking, and the intentional living of that sacred commitment—whether convenient or inconvenient—will radically change your heart, your mind, your attitude, and your relationships. Becoming fine tuned to the sure and subtle movements of the Holy Spirit requires an ongoing formation of conscience, an ongoing awakening to the necessary integrity of your being-in-God. Even becoming aware of the many subtle expressions of violence which crop up in self-talk or informal conversation, or in the most mundane moments of an ordinary day, or becoming aware of the violence that bombards us as entertainment or news, requires you to intentionally "turn down the volume" on the roar of life in order to bring the interior self back to center, back to the place of peace.

Formation of *personal* conscience is grounded in this ethic of peacemaking and the discipline of nonviolent engagement of heart, soul, mind, and strength in every dimension of your life. And in an outward vocational expression, the awakening of *social* conscience turns you toward the world with the eyes and mind and heart of Christ. The awakening of social conscience demands the discipline of your steadfast nonviolent and compassionate engagement in the affairs of your world.[64]

The deep interior work of peacemaking, including the deep conversional struggle that may accompany it, is worthy material for examination in the context of spiritual and vocational direction. The challenge of peacemaking may lie as close to home as one's marriage relationship, relationship with aging parents or with one's adult siblings or children,

---

[63] Paul VI insisted in his address for the Celebration of the Day of Peace, January 1, 1972, "If you want Peace, work for Justice" (http://www.vatican.va/holy_father/paul_vi/messages/ peace/ documents/hf_p-vi_mes_19711208_v-world-day-for-peace_en.html).

[64] An excellent resource on formation of social conscience is John Neafsey, *A Sacred Voice is Calling: Personal Vocation and Social Conscience* (Maryknoll, NY: Orbis, 2006). A fuller discussion of the formation of social conscience appears in the next chapter.

workplace relationships, or that annoying next-door neighbor. The conversional work of peacemaking, not surprisingly, demands the humbling, disarming work of forgiveness—perhaps most often forgiveness of oneself. All of this becomes worthy material in the holy conversation of spiritual direction.

Bringing It Home

1.What does this phrase mean to me personally, that *I* am anointed for a
   purpose? What purpose? How would I describe it?

2.How faithfully do I seem to be living this anointing? What can I point
   to as evidence?

3.What situations or relationships challenge me to be a peacemaker?
   Where does the work of peacemaking rank in my life?

4.Do I possess or actively cultivate the interior life and spirit of a
   peacemaker? How so?

Hold this Thought

I am allowing myself to be drawn increasingly

into the mystery of God.

WASHED, ANOINTED, FED, READY FOR WORK

Growing into a Life of Meaning

When I launched Awakening Vocations some years ago, I knew I was taking a risk in including the word "vocations" in the name of the organization. The word, for many church people, immediately evokes certain images and understandings which they perceive have no bearing on their life. Certainly within Catholic church circles the word "vocation" has most often referred to "a calling to priesthood" or "a calling to religious life." These professions—we might indeed call them "professions of faith"—have never been the statistical norm across the broader church population.

To speak honestly about the deeper and more broadly engaging dimensions of vocation, I have found it necessary to speak first about the nature of God's calling which springs from the one common font of Christian life, our baptism into Christ. Not surprisingly, in my spiritual and vocational direction practice the nature of God's calling is the topic most frequently brought for examination. Individuals who attend to the direction of their lives are seeking the words that will best express what they are experiencing in their journey through life, their journey into God.

Vocation Discernment: Someone Else's Work?

I know a young man, pious and devoted to a life of prayer, applying his intellectual best to his studies, open to God's movement in his life, with a beautiful heart for God's people. His passion is to move to a state in another part of the nation with chronically high poverty and incarceration rates, become a legal advocate for prisoners on death row, and press for life-sentence alternatives to the death penalty. I know a young woman, living chastely, reaching out to others in apostolic works, carrying the needs of the world in her prayer. She is completing her internship to serve the poor as a rural physician.

Why are these and other young, devout people, some of them single, some of them living an authentic and exemplary celibate life, not discerning a calling to priesthood or to religious life? They seem to have all the indicators.

Indeed. They also have all the indicators for living a fruitful and mature Christian life within a complex twenty-first century world. Some—most, perhaps—will enter into Christian married life, and others will embrace celibate life. And of these, some may enter into priesthood or consecrated religious life. Who is called into active service in the reign of God? *Every* man, *every* woman, *every* young adult, and *every* youth who has been initiated into Christian life—in other words, *every* one who has been washed, anointed, fed, and hopefully now stands ready for work.

Statistically and historically, the highest percentages of baptized men and women have entered into Christian married life. Of those who have not moved in the direction of marriage, not all have moved in the direction of priesthood or religious life. The vast majority of the baptized have remained "in the world" rather than pursued some form of service directly in the church. Given these patterns, over time "vocation" has come to be seen as something special, something rare, something surpassing the ordinary, a calling to a way of life set apart from the norm. The office of priest indeed is something set apart, with specific duties arising from a specific and particular presence of the risen Lord among his people. But what does this word "vocation" actually mean in its original and most generous Christian sense? How might we reclaim its application and power in ways that animate and sustain all who are baptized into Christ and anointed to be his presence in our world today?

Basics of Christian Vocation

The word *vocation* comes from the root word *voca*, meaning "to call." Vocation, for the baptized person, is a Spirit-led lifelong dynamic conversation —God's calling and your response. From the human standpoint vocation is always a *response,* not a choice. None of us is the initiator of our calling, God always is. Every human person—baptized Christian or not—is oriented toward a life of meaning and fulfillment because every human person is made in the image and likeness of God.[65] As a baptized individual you are oriented toward spiritual fruitfulness and effectiveness even more so, because the stirring of the Holy Spirit within you urges you to seek meaning, missional fulfillment, and the fullness of your unique personhood in God.[66]

In simplest terms, *vocation* means God's lifelong calling of you to the fullness of personhood according to the uniqueness of your being. Vocation is a core Gospel value to actualize the reign of God here and now, a core value and Christian imperative that applies to every baptized person in every state of life.

It is *God's* calling, it is *lifelong,* and it is a calling directed uniquely and lovingly to *you.* It is a calling perfectly suited to who you are, including your personality; your physical, mental, and emotional capacities; your talents, preferences, and spiritual gifts or charisms. And above all, God's calling is

---

[65] See Genesis 1:27.

[66] As St. Augustine famously wrote in his *Confessions*: "Our hearts are restless, Lord, until they rest in Thee."

perfectly suited to your unique role within the reign of God according to the circumstances and times in which you find yourself. Hence vocation discernment is the ongoing, ever evolving concern of every baptized person, in every state in life, from youth through all stages including old age.

By virtue of your being washed (in Baptism), anointed (in Confirmation), and fed (in Eucharist), you are fully called forth and disposed to be spiritually, mindfully, and emotionally equipped for worthy participation in the church's mission. How does this play out in the life of the baptized person?

Vocation is God's ultimately inescapable invitation to the particular ways of fulfilling God's purpose for your life. Think of this invitation as three-dimensional.[67] First, God's calling addresses *who* God desires you to be (your self-identity in God); second, God's calling addresses *how* you are to become that unique person (your vocational lifestyle); and third, God's calling addresses *what* you are called upon by God to do for the greater good—all expressions of the reign of God.

In this three-dimensional view of vocation, you are called upon by God to *be someone* before you are called upon by God to *do something*. This order of identity and activity is quite the opposite of what we often find in our culture, where "what we do" defines "who we are" in others' eyes—or even in our own.

Not surprisingly, your vocation is a unique expression of the church's vocation, which is, first, to enable every human being to encounter Jesus, and second, to transform institutions and cultures through the power of the risen Lord. You engage in this mission according to the ways that you have been anointed and gifted. And your calling is embedded within the mission of the Christian community.[68]

Finally, your vocation is both *eternal* and *temporal*.[69] Your eternal

---

[67] See Nemeck and Coombs, *Called by God,* esp. 2, 108–109.

[68] See *Pastoral Constitution on the Church in the Modern World;* see also *CCC,* para. 2030.

[69] See Nemeck and Coombs, *Called by God,* ch. 8, esp. p. 73.

vocation is to everlasting communion in the intimate life of the Father, the Son, and the Holy Spirit. This everlasting communion has been God's desiring from the beginning, and this experience of human-divine communion is not only the goal in the afterlife but something to be experienced and savored here and now. This eternal dimension of vocation is most serenely illustrated in the sacred icon, *Holy Trinity,* written by the fifteenth century Russian monk Andrei Rublev. At the divine banquet table where the three figures sit,[70] one space for a fourth guest is open in the foreground, a place at this holy table which is reserved for the viewer. This open space is your space. To claim and actually take that place reserved for you at the divine banquet is to live—here and now—your eternal calling, your eternal vocation. Ultimately your calling is to a fullness of presence in the divine Presence. As the Psalmist proclaims: "You will show me the path to life, / abounding joy in your presence, / the delights at your right hand forever" (Psalm 16:11).

Your temporal vocation unfolds in space and time, in the particular circumstances of your life, and in reflection upon God's movement in your life. This "temporal vocation" is what most of us have in mind when we ask, "What am I supposed to do with my life? What is my vocation?" Of course, the vocational answer to these questions has no direction or purpose or means of effectiveness outside the all-encompassing context of God's eternal calling of you into intimate and everlasting communion.

In our hurry-up-and-claim-it-now culture we oftentimes find it tempting to default to the "doing" mode when the less results-driven "being" mode is really what generates, guides, and sustains our moving in God's direction. These vocational aspects of your life are not only worthy but necessary topics for conversation in spiritual and vocational direction. Vocation, at heart, is about relationship and the particular and gifted expressions of the relation of self with God and therefore relation of self with others and with the

---

[70] Representing the three messengers who visited Abraham and Sarah (see Genesis 18:1–15) who are understood to forefigure the Holy Trinity. See Henri J. M. Nouwen, *Behold the Beauty of the Lord: Praying with Icons* (Notre Dame, IN: Ave Maria, 1987, 2002), 19–27. See also my essay titled "Meditation on Three Words," in *Touching the Reign of God*, 50–55.

world.

What's in Your Spiritual Toolkit?

If you are employed, or even deeply engaged in a particular career, you most likely did not "just show up," unprepared for the assignment. You may have gone to school, undergone specific training, interned and developed specific skills, built a résumé or portfolio of accomplishments, and perhaps even acquired advanced degrees. You may possess the perfect personality and temperament for your work. These are all things that make up your professional toolkit.

Similarly we can speak of a spiritual toolkit. Before you pursue a field of study or a line of work, or as you begin to apprentice yourself to a certain calling or craft, you discover certain inclinations toward these things, or a certain ease or effectiveness that attracts or engages you in the first place. You begin to discover evidence of spiritual gifts, or charisms.

Charism is a Greek term meaning a gift or ability, given by the Holy Spirit, in order to accomplish what you could not accomplish merely by talent or skill, and meant to be shared generously for the good of others. How do you know what's in your spiritual toolkit? Spiritual gifts inventories abound. One spiritual gifts inventory, which is part of the "Called and Gifted" workshop of the Catherine of Siena Institute,[71] stands out for the rich theological foundation on which it rests. The "Called and Gifted" workshop presents a solid theological understanding of the work of the Holy Spirit through the charisms in a way that enables you to identify and connect your gifts with the world's need. This theological foundation is necessary to actually make sense of the charisms and their distinctive role in the life of baptized men and women.

If you are baptized, you already have a spiritual toolkit amply stocked with the charisms you need to fulfill God's plan for the portion of today's world

---

[71] See www.siena.org.

which you uniquely touch. That world may be within the walls of your home, or it may be in the public sphere, the workplace, the classroom, or on the international stage. But merely possessing such a spiritual toolkit is not the same as actually knowing what these charisms are, how they work in general, and how they are expressed uniquely in your life.

Unfortunately, many spiritual direction programs still lack adequate curriculum and practice in charism discernment or understanding of the theological and vocational implications of charism discernment in the spiritual direction setting. As a spiritual and vocational director I find listening for evidence of charisms to be indispensable in guiding directees to discover and to discern God's fine-tuned movement in their life.

The point of charism discernment is not merely to know what spiritual gifts you possess. In a very real sense you do not "possess" the charisms, nor do you choose them. Over time you discover that these charisms have, in a sense, chosen you. You live at the service of these expressions of the Holy Spirit for the good of others. Rather, the point of charism discernment is to make sense of why your life is the way it is *because* of the charisms that you have been given, and to recognize patterns of God's movement in your life through the use of your particular cluster of charisms. This ability to identify the patterns of effectiveness in your life is key to understanding God's unique purpose for your life and God's unique work of love expressed through you for the sake of the world. In other words, when you can clearly identify charisms at work in your life you can begin to understand your vocation.

Finding a Life of Meaning

By its very source—God's desiring the wholeness of personhood and fullness of life for each individual—vocation is inclusive, calling forth all who are baptized to a life of meaning, to share in the redemptive work of the risen Lord. For the baptized and anointed, this life of meaning is the living expression of true freedom—not a freedom to do as you please (which might better be termed *license*)—but freedom to do that which, at the core of your being, you find you *must* do to most fully be your authentic self-in-God.[72] The only real human freedom is the freedom to experience, or at least initially to wholeheartedly seek and move toward, your unique personhood in God— whether you can name this experience or the Object of your seeking, or not. We call this interior freedom "authentic freedom."

Authentic freedom is the freedom to turn fully toward God, especially in the midst of complex circumstances, to be uniquely God's image in these particular circumstances, for these particular others at this particular time. Authentic freedom is a freedom which is both interior and embodied, the inward and the outward together expressing one's calling. In this sense vocation is Incarnational—giving your own flesh and voice and presence to the risen Lord here and now.

As human beings, among our deepest longings we experience a longing for communities of meaning and an abiding experience of belonging. By our very nature we want to belong, to be included.[73] Ideally, for the baptized man or woman the community of meaning is first and foremost the Christian community, the Eucharistic community, the place of gathering for true spiritual sustenance. In Christian community we encounter the Lord's own deep-rooted concern for life, justice, mercy, and peace—not only for ourselves and our loved ones, but for those beyond the borders of our immediate concern.

---

[72] I think here of Etty Hillesum, a young Jewish woman living in Nazi-occupied Amsterdam. She knew her fate and in her journal she wrote: "Very well then … I accept it. … I work and continue to live with the same conviction and I find life meaningful." From *An Interrupted Life: The Diaries of Etty Hillesum, 1941–1943* (New York: Pantheon, 1983), in Ellsberg, *All Saints,* 522. Her "work" was tending day and night to the anguish of family members, friends, and strangers in the camp, with endless compassion expressed in practical deeds of comfort and assistance. She was not a baptized Christian, but in her "interrupted life" we find a powerful expression of an "authentic self-in-God." Clearly God's gifts are not limited to the baptized.

[73] Ironically, as noted earlier, electronic social networking, which appears to form "community," oftentimes becomes an isolating vicarious striving to "connect," and can lack the capacity to create an experience of community that can sustain the human spirit in any meaningful way.

Where Conscience Fits In

We live in a world that desperately needs the Eucharistic imagination and generosity, the healing, the peace, and the redeeming love of God. God's calling in your life, you begin to discover, is not just to meaningful work that fulfills you, but is a calling to a way of being wholeheartedly and generously present to a complex and deeply hurting world. Vocation, you begin to realize, is about standing compassionately, intentionally, and wholeheartedly in the place of Jesus. You discover that you really are on a mission which is larger than yourself. You begin to understand in a new light that your life really is no longer your own, as St. Paul insists, but in fact does belong to Christ.[74]

This deeper level of interior awakening is absolutely necessary if you are to mature spiritually. The discovery of the deeper and more self-involving response to God's calling is the starting point for formation of social conscience.[75] You begin to realize more deeply that your journey into holiness includes not only you but all those whose lives you touch, including those whose lives may seem a burden to you.[76] Your journey into holiness includes, too, those whose cries reach your ears, whose suffering and crushing indignities you cannot ignore, whether they are in your broader community or in another part of the world.

This awakening to God's deeper calling occurs in the course of

---

[74] See 1 Corinthians 6:19–20: "[Y]ou are not your own[.] For you have been purchased at a price." See also Colossians 3:3: "For you have died, and your life is hidden with Christ in God"; see also 2 Corinthians 5:15: "He indeed died for all, so that those who live might no longer live for themselves but for him who for their sake died and was raised."

[75] See Neafsey, *A Sacred Voice is Calling.*

[76] Dorothy Day wrote of the cantankerous old Mr. O'Connell who took up residence on the Catholic Worker farm: "We were being pruned, all right. ... I would look upon Maurice with gratitude and with pity, that God should choose him to teach us such lessons. ... I have faith, that Maurice O'Connell ... was an instrument chosen by God to make us grow in wisdom and faith and love." Quoted in Robert Ellsberg, ed., *Dorothy Day: Selected Writings* (Maryknoll, NY: Orbis, 1983, 1992), 131–132.

faithfully contemplating the Scriptures,[77] faithfully listening to your heart where God speaks, and faithfully listening, too, to the voice of those who suffer. They may live within your household, be camped out at the edges of your town, or their faces may be fleeting images on the evening news. Sometimes those who suffer will be in the alleys of your inner city; sometimes they will be in countries you cannot readily locate on the map. The world's anguish will become your teacher, discipling you in the difficult and painful lesson that real commitment to life, justice, mercy, and peacemaking is more than a concept and more than a rallying cry. Real commitment is action based on your being in this particular place at this particular time, anointed and responsive for the purpose of revealing the reign of God in ways that you perhaps have not yet imagined. You will find yourself putting your own skin in the game, and possibly leaving a pint of blood, sweat, and tears on the floor. The awakening of social conscience is a crucial step in the irreversible process of throwing your life away for the sake of the Gospel.

As theologian Jon Sobrino writes,[78] awakening to your social conscience means awakening *from* "the sleep of inhumanity" and awakening *to* God's dream for humankind and all of creation. The awakening of social conscience, both personally and collectively, indeed is the necessary first step toward fulfillment of the reign of God which Jesus poses in his instruction on the last judgment: "For I was hungry and you gave me food, I was thirsty and you gave me drink, a stranger and you welcomed me, naked and you clothed me, ill and you cared for me, in prison and you visited me" (Matthew 25:35–36).

Exploring where you are in your own process of the awakening of social conscience is a deeper work of spiritual and vocational direction. This is the necessary and sometimes affirming, oftentimes painful conversation of self with the soul, a conversation best guided by the wise counsel of accountability

---

[77] Good starting points for entry into the Scriptures are the Book of Psalms and two portions of the Gospel of St. Matthew: the inaugural sermon (chaps. 5–7) and the Judgment of the Nations (25:31–46).

[78] Jon Sobrino, SJ, *The Principle of Mercy: Taking the Crucified People from the Cross* (Maryknoll, NY: Orbis, 1994), 1, in Neafsey, *A Sacred Voice is Calling,* 146.

and hope. This awakening of social conscience sometimes happens in increments, and sometimes in a seeming instant, in a searing flash of moral insight, when you are confronted with the immediacy of human anguish coupled with stirrings of your own capacity to respond. Those stirrings, sometimes so compelling that you know that you cannot walk away, are not of you but of the Holy Spirit, urging you toward the necessary actions to connect your gifts with others' need, for the healing of the world in some particular way. You may sense more inadequacies than brilliant successes as you try to live with the heart of God in the midst of an agitated world. The awakening of social conscience will put you on the path of humility and radical trust in God, and impel you on a lifelong journey of justice, mercy, and divine peacemaking.

Vocations that Touch the World

As you mature in your discernment of the ways God is calling you to fullness of personhood and to grow more seriously into your particular patterns of effectiveness in your life, you will begin to integrate your inner world of faith and meaning with the larger world in which you live. The relationships and commitments which connect you with the world outside yourself give actual shape and voice and presence to God's particular desiring and your lifelong nuanced response. An interior shift occurs. "Making sure everything is right with *my* world" gradually becomes "making sure everything is right with *our* world." A clear sense of responsibility begins to emerge, expressed through an actual engagement with the world which brings healing, hope, and a freedom that enables the world to be its better self. No one of us can heal the wounds and solve the problems of the entire world, but each one of us has been anointed and gifted to do something compassionate and life-affirming in the world we touch.

I once met a small town elementary teacher who explained why he turned down the offer of a better paying school administrator job. His reason? "I work with children from extremely poor families who live in dreary, unwelcoming, and very unstable home environments," he said. "My greatest joy is to welcome each child by name each day into a happy classroom." His unmistakable charism of Hospitality compels him to welcome, each day, into the safe circle of God's embrace these small-town, resource-poor children who most need to feel included.

I know an oncology surgeon with an unusual ability to diagnose tumors that fail to show up in sophisticated tests. This surgeon does not practice in some large, prestigious medical center, although she easily could, and she easily could bring home a handsome salary. Rather, she works in an unpretentious regional hospital. "There seems to be a knowing in my hands," she says. "I receive referrals from doctors all across the region. What eludes them, even after extensive diagnostic scans, I seem able to quickly find." She possesses the diagnostic charism of Wisdom.

My friend Sister Margaret, in her mid-nineties and with not a penny to her name, is well known for her ability to walk into a room, talk about her work with the imprisoned and the poor, and walk away with checks and cash filling her pockets to directly support her many outreach ministries. She has a charism of Giving.

My father, a small-town barber, often went on his day off to the homes of his longtime customers, older gents who had become homebound or bedridden, to cut their hair and freshen them up, to make them feel like they still possessed human dignity, to feel as though their diminished lives still mattered. My father touched the lives of many in our little town, in hidden and quite ordinary ways, through the charism of Mercy.

God does not ask for heroics, but for attentiveness, or "real presence." And God asks for faithfulness—faithfulness in a threefold way: faithfulness to God's willing, faithfulness to those you encounter, and faithfulness to the gifts you have been given to generously share. Any "heroics" that others might perceive in you are not of your own doing but are expressions of the Holy Spirit at work in your life. There is no such thing as a life without a vocation, nor is there any such thing as a vocation that does not touch the world.

A Life Awakened

Ultimately, what is the desired outcome of spiritual and vocational direction? It is a life awakened to God, a life awakened, as Sobrino says, from the sleep of inhumanity, a life awakened and fearlessly present to the truth of its purpose and beauty. When the director and directee move together in God's direction, the directee becomes liberated *from* obstacles to wholeness and holiness, and liberated *for* action according to divine purpose and the particular expressions of one's anointing.

When you move in God's direction you become spiritually alive and gracefully animated in the Holy Spirit for that divine purpose which you will more deeply understand and appreciate over time. And when you are animated in the Holy Spirit you become spiritually fruitful—not necessarily as *you* had imagined fruitfulness, but as *God* eternally imagines your fruitfulness and wholeness of being. You become spiritually fruitful not by any efforts of your own—just as a tree does not bear fruit through its own initiative. Rather, you become fruitful by virtue of your spiritual roots firmly held in the good soil of God's willing and God's desiring. As Jesus assured his followers, "I am the vine, you are the branches. Whoever remains in me and I in [them] will bear much fruit, because without me you can do nothing" (John 15:5).

The Holy Spirit awakens, liberates, and animates in countless ways, in part through the holy conversation of spiritual and vocational direction. And while the Holy Spirit is the true director and animator within this holy conversation, some things are required personally of you, as directee, prior to and flowing from that conversation.

First, you must *"show up."* Mature spiritual work requires you to be intentionally and wholeheartedly present to your life, your relationships, your commitments, and all the inner work which these key dimensions of your life entail. None of us is fully there, yet each of us must strive. Continually you will find the invitation and the opportunity to cultivate and nudge forward your ability to notice things—to notice what you hear, and what you see, to notice what you touch, and what you feel interiorly.

Second, you will increasingly encounter the invitation and the challenge to *lean into God* with radical trust. We live in a culture that has perfected and elevated chronic worry to a high art. Hence, it is important to honestly ask yourself, "Is my prayer time more accurately my opportunity to get down into the worry zone?" Worry and anxiety are serious obstacles to authentic prayer and to any authentic engagement in life. They deaden the possibility of your being authentically present to your life. Jesus was quite clear about the insidious nature of worry and anxiety and fear: "Do *not* be afraid; have *faith* in God," he urged repeatedly, "and *faith* in me." His words were simple and direct. He clearly meant what he said, and your challenge is to take his words to heart and live your life, especially in its more challenging dimensions, with holy courage.

Third, a life awakened requires you to *act*. You have been anointed to touch the world—your world—with the real though hidden presence of the risen Lord. If the path or course of action which you have chosen is moving you in a direction not of God's desiring, you will learn soon enough how to redirect your course in order to move gracefully in God's direction. God is not interested in your grieving over failure or lost time.

Finally, in all things, *pray*. Expand your capacity to depend on God, and to wait expectantly on God's movement and the promptings of the Holy Spirit. Learn to trust, to really *trust,* the relationship. Like a well-practiced dance partner, learn to read the clues to the next step contained in the subtle movements of the present step, so that the two of you—yourself and the Holy Spirit—can flow like a graceful *one* across the terrain of your life.

Finding Vocational Joy

For many people as they launch into their morning commute, the words *joy* and *work* might not be two words that they would easily pair in the same sentence. In times when companies and major institutions and government agencies recoil from the sting of economic recession, many people who find themselves employed feel grateful simply to have a job, any job. Yet Jesus' ardent prayer was that *in our lifetime* we might know abundant goodness and share in his joy completely. "I came," we hear him say, "so that [you] might have life and have it more abundantly" (John 10:10); and again, "Until now you have not asked anything in my name; ask and you will receive, so that your joy may be complete" (John 16:24). Jesus was speaking of a deep abiding vocational joy, the joy of remaining secure within his Father's calling and becoming his visible presence in this world in ways that are perfectly suited to our lives and to our happiness.

Vocational joy is more than liking what you do for a living. Vocational joy goes far deeper than that. It is the joy of knowing that you are called by God to be fully alive in the life that has your name on it. Even in the midst of challenge you begin to experience a joy that springs from the core of your being, an existential joy that radiates outward to all the dimensions and endeavors of your life. Vocational joy can infuse your current work circumstances even as you might acknowledge that where you are presently is no longer the right fit. Vocational joy is not rooted in the circumstances of your work life but in your being-in-God.

Vocational joy is the unmistakable indicator that you are becoming who you are anointed to be in God, and that you are doing what you have been anointed to do. First of all, this means abiding in the Father's love, standing in the place of Jesus in the ways you have been uniquely gifted, in this place and time, in these particular circumstances. A current unfulfilling job is not "forever." For those who are moving in God's direction, an unfulfilling job may be the irritating sand in the oyster that eventually produces the pearl. Always seek the pearl, Jesus admonishes, especially the pearl of great price.[79] When you experience vocational joy you know you are shifting *from maintenance,* or "life

---

[79] See Matthew 13:46.

as usual," *to mission,* or a more wholehearted participation in the mystery of God's plan.

And what is this mission? Quite simply, your mission is to enable every person you encounter to actually encounter Jesus himself, and, along with the larger company of God's anointed ones, to transform institutions and cultures through the risen Lord who draws all things to himself.[80] Carefully note the wording here: The first part of your mission is not to bring every person into the church, but to enable each person you meet to encounter Jesus through you, where they are, in whatever circumstances they find themselves, and in whatever degree of readiness they might be for such an encounter.

The second part of the vocational mission speaks directly to the world of work, of advocacy, and to every kind of human encounter and human endeavor: to transform institutions and cultures—seldom single-handedly but rather, through the persistent united advocacy and effort that comes from participating in the community of the Beloved and the larger community. Baptized men and women in every arena—in all levels of government and public service, law, health care, education, human services, banking, insurance, the sciences, agriculture, the arts and entertainment, and all areas of human and social concern—are anointed to engage a world in need of the light of the risen Lord and the animating leaven of the Holy Spirit.

This vocational journey sounds noble and energizing and worthy of your best efforts. But the truth is that regular reflection on how you are living this mission, and the quality of your accountability for this mission, deserves the guidance of a trusted other—a guide, a mentor, a spiritual or vocational director. In fact, regular reflection on personal mission is vital for spiritual directors, too. Such personal reflection leads to attentiveness, conversion, insight, and encouragement—all important qualities which the Holy Spirit brings to the ongoing conversation of spiritual and vocational direction.

---

[80] See John 12:32. See also Colossians 1:20: "and through [Christ] to reconcile all things, ... / making peace by the blood of his cross."

1.How would I describe a life of meaning as I actually experience it? Does this life which I currently experience feel big enough, and true enough, and reflective of my baptismal anointing? Now so?

2.What events, or life circumstances, or encounters have initiated or further advanced my awakening of social conscience? How has this awakening brought vocational direction to my life?

3.When do I experience vocational joy in my life? What am I doing in these moments?

4.What patterns of effectiveness seem to be evident or emerging in my life or in my work?

Hold this Thought

My life gains deeper meaning as I mature

in my anointing in Christ.

9

LIVING YOUR CALLING RESPONSIBLY

Vocational Discernment in a Nutshell

Stopped at an intersection one day, I noticed the bumper sticker on the car ahead of me. It drew my attention like a bug to a zap light. It read: "What if the hokey pokey really is what it's all about?" My first response was an interior groan, followed by the dreaded thought that I might have that goofy song in my head all day. As I waited for the light to change I began to play with the message. Being a wordsmith, I wondered, "Where does that phrase *hokey pokey* come from?"

Hokey pokey, it turns out, is a corruption of the phrase *hocus-pocus*, an arbitrary formula attributed to medieval traveling scholars; in short, it refers to the meaningless words that were used as a spell of sorts by conjurers. Hocus-pocus, in fact, was pretty much what non-Latin speaking common folk in the pews, back in those medieval days, understood as the words of consecration, from which that phrase originates: *hoc est enim Corpus meum.* "This is my Body, which is given for you." These words we hold as sacred, coming from the lips of the Lord himself, as recorded in Scripture, spoken on the night before he died, words that form the center of our Eucharistic celebrations. These words bring us to the very core of Jesus' own calling. These words, *Hoc est enim Corpus meum,* reveal Jesus' profoundly vocational giving of self, unconditionally, not only for the good of others but for the redemption—blood purchase—of all of humankind, the redeeming of all of creation.

Living as Though the Truth were True

Thinking back to that bumper sticker, I find that the question now rightly becomes: What if *Hoc est enim Corpus meum* really is what it's all about? As baptized men and women we profess that this redemptive self-offering indeed *is* "what it's all about." God has done some serious high-stakes investing in the likes of you and me. In the book of Revelation the elders sing: "Worthy are you ... / for you were slain and with your blood you purchased for God / those from every tribe and tongue, people and nation" (Revelation 5:9). This hymn echoes the words of St. Paul, who writes of Christ Jesus who "emptied himself, / taking the form of a slave, / coming in human likeness; / ... [yet] he humbled himself, / becoming obedient to death. ... / Because of this, God greatly exalted him" (Philippians 2:6–9a).

These words capture Jesus' vocational fulfillment, extolling the One who took his calling and anointing and mission to be true.

Vocationally, what do these words of selfless outpouring mean for your life? Only you can answer this question. Your work as you mature in the course of your life is to sit attentively with these words, own them, appropriate them to your circumstances; apply them as the filter through which you experience your life here and now, and through which, equally, you engage in the concerns of your world. The divine calling, invitation, and challenge is to live, in the words of Jesuit peace activist Daniel Berrigan, "as though the truth were true."[81]

Not only was Jesus' life among us—including his passion, death, and

---

[81] Daniel Berrigan, SJ, quoted in John Neafsey, *A Sacred Voice is Calling,* 51.

resurrection—God's high-stakes investment in this world. *Your* life equally is God's high-stakes investment in this world. You are the only one who can give life to the words "This is my body, which is given for you" in your own particular life's narrative. But you do not have to undertake this task unaided. The task is nothing less than living your baptism responsibly, a work worthy of deep reflection on the Gospel and the guidance of a wise mentor or director. "Anyone who wants to live their baptism responsibly," counsels Benedict XVI, "should have a spiritual director."[82] Why? Benedict compares spiritual direction to that spiritually intimate and formative bond between Jesus and his disciples which oriented them and indeed impelled them toward the Father's willing.

Living your calling responsibly in the world will always contain a challenge because it will lead you to fullness of life-in-God by way of the cross, by way of an unavoidable surrender of self to the mystery of God's perfect willing. A Christ-centered spiritual and vocational director who understands this imperative will keep you focused, centered, and honest. The full-pledge investment in your life has already been made. No matter where you are in your life right now—moving in God's direction or resisting, God would make that investment in you all over again, in a heartbeat.

The Danger of Choosing a Vocation

Many young people in the church today feel the pressure to "choose a vocation." This pressure to "hurry up and choose" parallels the pressure that young people experience more broadly throughout our culture, a pressure to settle on an academic major, or get a career focus, or find that right person to marry, often not because *they* feel compelled to do so, or because the time is right, but because others who influence their lives feel an anxiety about the next generation making the right and prudent choices. In church circles, sadly, many *children* feel this pressure for vocational choice making. In the context of

---

[82] For Benedict XVI's address to the faculty of the Carmelite Institute of Spiritual Formation, the Teresianum, Rome, see www.catholicanchor.org/wordpress/archives/4246 (accessed June 4, 2011).

church, many men and women who find themselves "still unmarried" but of an "investable" age—up to, say, age 40 or so—often feel the strong encouragement to choose a vocation to one of "the big three"—priesthood, religious life, or marriage—as though choosing one of these options would somehow prove that you can still fit in somewhere.

Vocation is God's lifelong and intimately personal calling of each individual to the fullness of personhood. Vocation, or this wholehearted engagement in God's calling, is no more an option to one's spiritual life than breath is to one's physical life. Vocation is not for the few but is a Gospel value that applies to every baptized person in every state and stage of life. The two great teachings of Jesus, found in St. Matthew's Gospel—the Sermon on the Mount[83] and the parable of the Judgment of the Nations[84]—reinforce the understanding that each of us is particularly called upon by God to reveal the reign of God in the oftentimes unfavorable and challenging circumstances of life. God calls upon each of us not broadly or generally, and certainly not capriciously, but with great loving care and equally loving design—for your own life and for those whose lives you will touch.

God's calling can never be forced upon you, because God's calling is perfectly suited to who you are and who you are designed to most fully become. Nor can any outside forces justly convince you to *choose* one way of life over another.[85] To do so, no matter how well intentioned, is a form of violence to the integrity of one's personhood. Nor can you select the calling of your choice. If God has formed you for a mission in life that you have not yet imagined, be

---

[83] See Matthew 5–7.

[84] See Matthew 25:31–46.

[85] This is not to say that parents, teachers, or other mentors or elders have no influence or authority to guide a young person in growth in moral virtue or in "checking out" one interest or another, one path of studies or Christian lifestyle or work or another. But freedom of personhood, even of the young, must be defended as the soul and mind and heart are formed by larger, more hidden forces—the deeper workings of the Holy Spirit within the individual.

ready to let go all lesser dreams and move in God's direction.[86] Moving in God's direction according to God's unique calling of you is the only real path to your authentic happiness.

Your vocation—or your lifelong journey into the fullness of your personhood—is bestowed by God. Thankfully, God does not rely on statistics, projections, or industry trends, nor does God consider spreadsheet probabilities or recession-proof career options to determine how you can best reveal the reign of God. In short, God simply says, "Trust me." And the author of the Letter to the Hebrews affirms: *The one who made the promise is worthy of the trust.*[87]

While your vocation is bestowed by God, it also is called forth and affirmed, sometimes by those who know you most intimately, sometimes by the Christian community, and sometimes by the broader community which you touch. Whether understood as such or intuited based on a consistent pattern of encouragements, this calling forth is the work of the Holy Spirit active in others, affirming in you what God already has set in motion, even if only in a hidden or incipient way.

Finally, God's calling must be actively cultivated by you, examined, tested, tried. And because God's calling is always a divine desire for your coming to fullness of your unique personhood, that calling is going to evolve, unfold, and mature over time. Which means that God's calling is going to look somewhat different—or sometimes astonishingly different—as you mature. Given this unfolding quality of God's calling, it is especially helpful to have a vocational guide or spiritual director who can sit attentively with you as you decipher and find context for your evolving relationship with God and the particulars of God's movement in your life. Moving in God's direction in new ways does not mean that you must betray or jettison your past. It means that God is up to something new, acting at the frontier of your life, and your work is to

---

[86] St. Paul's words have vocational meaning here, recalling the words of the prophet Isaiah: "What eye has not seen, and ear has not heard, / and what has not entered the human heart, / what God has prepared for those who love him" (1 Corinthians 2:9; see Isaiah 64:3).

[87] See Hebrews 11:11.

pay attention to what is happening now.[88]

Your Real Vocation

Your fundamental vocation is, and will always be, to *life in Christ.* Your vocation is not first about *doing something,* but about *being someone*— specifically, being your authentic self-in-God.[89] For the man or woman of Christian faith, faithfulness and obedience are two lifelong expressions of the authentic self: *faithfulness* to God and *listening openly* with the ear of the heart (which is the root of this word *obedience*) to the needs of the world around you. The great consolation is this: Your life began in God; you will be completely God's in the end; and no part of your life escapes God's loving claim. Your work is to live as though these things are true—because they are. Living with this awareness of the vocational trajectory of your life is what it means to live your life in Christ. You do not set the trajectory; God does. This may be one of the most important awakenings you will experience in the process of growing into God's calling of you.

All of human life flows from God and is fulfilled in God. Indeed, every human person, all of humankind, and all of creation flows from God and is fulfilled in God, through the risen Christ.[90] Your coming to fullest expression of your personhood does not hinge on what *you* choose, but on what God already has chosen for you for the utter perfection of your life and for the good of the

---

[88] This vocational "paying attention" to what God is doing illustrates the challenge of Isaiah's words: "See, I am doing something new! / Now it springs forth, do you not perceive it?" (Isaiah 43:19).

[89] I recently met with a woman who had left a long-time employment which had drained life and spirit out of her pretty much from the first week. As we talked about her future she became animated by real possibilities that would call upon her best talents and interests. "The only obstacle is the negative self-talk that keeps popping up in my head," she said. "No matter how hard I try to get rid of it, it keeps coming back." I said to her, "Perhaps it is trying to tell you something, a message for you which you have not yet received. Invite the negative self-talk into conversation. Listen to what it is trying to say; ask it for a blessing, and then let it go."

[90] See Colossians 1:16: "For in him were created all things in heaven and on earth, / the visible and the invisible, / ... all things were created through him and for him."

world you touch.

You indeed are called by God because God still desires to touch, heal, and transform the world in unique ways through you as part of the body of Christ. How you will move in God's direction over the course of your life may take many forms and expressions. Openness to God's willing, and really trusting that God's willing for your life and for the life of the world ultimately cannot be thwarted, is absolutely necessary—an expression of absolute trust that allows no room for fear.[91]

Unconditional and expectant openness to God's willing is deeply spiritual work. It also can be emotionally wrenching work, especially if you are prone to fear or to worry, or if you seek to be in control at all times of the path your life takes. Unconditional openness to God's willing has a direct and immediate impact on attitude, expectations, and the ability to act effectively.

Your capacity for openness to God is worthy material to bring to conversation in the course of spiritual and vocational direction.

Security versus Risk

Personality has something to do with how you will move in God's direction. Some people can be described as steady, deep-rooted, steadfast in their commitments, perhaps even long-suffering and faithful to conditions or commitments from which others would sooner flee. Consistency, constancy, faithfulness to what is given—these are words that often describe those who are most given to a sure and steady path in life.

Other people can be described as open to change and to experimenting

---

[91] In the darkest period of his life Blessed John Henry Cardinal Newman wrote, "God has determined, unless I interfere with His plan, that I should reach that which will be my greatest happiness. He looks on me individually, He calls me by my name, He knows what I can do, what I can best be, what is my greatest happiness, and He means to give it to me." From Meditation 299 (1), "Hope in God-Creator," March 6, 1848, http://www.newmanreader.org/works/meditations/meditations9.html#doctrine1 (accessed July 15, 2011).

with what is new or untried. They have a capacity for new information, and are able to bring fresh context to commitments when conditions change or desired opportunities open up. They know their spiritual base and they experience it as a platform for what God is still revealing. Openness, interior agility, faithfulness to a larger horizon—these are words that often describe those who are not shaken by risk but rather are quite at home with it. When Peter challenged Jesus to call him to walk across the stormy waters, Jesus issued the simple invitation: "Come." We see this man Peter intentionally move from the physical security of the boat and the emotional security of friends caught in a dangerous predicament to the unimaginably risky business of defying the laws of physics and walking to his Lord across the water. And for a moment he apparently perceived himself worthy of the invitation.

"Vocational security" is a nonsense phrase. (Truth be told, "job security" is a nonsense phrase, too.) At some point in our lives Jesus says, "Come" to every one of us. There is no such thing as a baptized man or woman who can escape or honestly maneuver around this gut-wrenching, life-shaping invitation of the crucified and risen Lord. In response to the invitation we can do one of two things: We can trust that the invitation is real, let go the security of what has held our life together so far, and walk among the waves with our eyes fixed on the One who beckons us. Or, we can distrust the Lord's invitation and drown in our own sea of doubt.

God's calling always carries risk—just look at Jesus as he submitted to his arrest, mock trial, scourging, and execution. In his final hours the one relationship which had sustained him all his life now escaped him. Betrayal by others, even those closest to us, or even feeling betrayed by a hope or a dream, is an integral part of human experience. The sting of betrayal may be one of God's ways of testing to see where our vocational roots really lie. Pursuit of God's calling carries inescapable risk.

But not every risk we encounter in life flows from God's calling. Some risks can arise from mere foolishness on our part, from not paying attention to warning signs and to changing conditions. *God does not set us up to fail.* God has no interest in our failure, but does have a passionate interest in our getting things gracefully right. Developing the ability to distinguish God's calling from, say, restless intuitions, is a deep work of spiritual and vocational direction.

The Work of Vocational Discernment

Not all of life is a storm. Not all of life tosses you to the edge of your boat, nor hurls you to the precipice where life as you have known it simply drops off. Yet every one of us encounters those invitations, those challenges, which take us beyond the known borders of our lives. The invitation might lie in the conference you attend that reframes your previous knowledge or understanding in an entirely new light. Or the challenge might be the new employment or the new assignment that tests your stamina beyond what you thought you had in you. These invitations and challenges come in every stage in life. Indeed, if we allow them, they actually help to shape each stage of our lives.

How do you mesh the immediate realities of daily life with the ultimate realities of your life in God? These are not two separate worlds but one, where divine realities are expressed through the human, the ordinary, the mundane, the needful. As St. Paul says, "We hold this treasure [of God] in earthen vessels."[92] The challenge of Christian faith is to contain the infinite and everlasting within the cramped quarters of the finite and temporal. Yet this amazing gift is what we are given as the starting point in our spiritual life. How do you mesh the temporal with the eternal, the finite with the infinite?

First, you can ask yourself: What *patterns of experience and effectiveness* seem already to be evident, or at least emerging, in my life? What opportunities seem to keep coming up? What is the recurring word? What is the recurring message? Who is the interior visitor who keeps coming to the door of my mind, to the threshold of my intuition, coming to the door of my heart, and

---

[92] See 2 Corinthians 4:6.

whom, perhaps, I keep dismissing? You even may have a recurring dream that hangs in your memory like an unsolved puzzle. Pay attention to these patterns and opportunities and unbidden visitors. Notice what energizes you or gives you the feeling that the Holy Spirit is up to something and is already at work in you, even if you cannot name it.

Second, find ways to *lessen the impact of obstacles and negative factors* as you discern God's movement in your life. Were you told as a child that you would never amount to very much? Acknowledge it, bless it, and let it go. Did you pick up the notion that whatever you do in life, it won't make much difference? Bless that notion and let it go. Do you sabotage God's lovely desiring with unlovely habits and patterns of behavior? Do others perceive you, due to past failures, as "damaged goods"? Were you deprived of the opportunities that others may have taken for granted? Acknowledge all of these hurtful messages and experiences; bless them, and let them go. Just let them go. Take care of any unfinished business regarding forgiveness, drop the need to be right, and get on with *your* life, the only life you have been given, the life for which you have been anointed.

Indicators of Mature Vocational Awareness

Getting a clear picture of God's desiring for your life never comes all at once and seldom comes early. Few of us will ever experience a "road to Damascus" moment where vocational clarity comes like a lightning flash.[93] Coming to mature vocational awareness is more about the gradual process of waking up than it is about drama. You will, however, find indicators along the way that you are on the right path, through opportunities that open up, through experiences of being unusually effective without undue strain, or through prayerful reflection on patterns of God's movement in your life. The spiritual direction process can be especially helpful here, as you reflect on four major indicators of mature vocational awareness, as proposed by Nemeck and

---

[93] See Acts 9:1–9 for an account of the persecutor Saul's dramatic conversion.

Coombs.[94]

The first indicator of mature vocational awareness is an *existential inability to be otherwise, or to become or do otherwise.* Here you may become aware of a persistent urging at the core of your being to give yourself over completely to becoming whom you cannot resist becoming. You might take the plunge and go back to school for more specialized studies. You might respond to a friend's invitation to get involved in a faith initiative addressing social concerns. Or you might step forward in other ways, discovering that you are no longer capable of complacency.

The second indicator of mature vocational awareness is a *movement from relationship with God as "friend" to relationship with God as "Mystery."* As the interior self matures the relationship with God becomes more silent, more loving, and more deeply trusting. The restless pushback eventually resolves into a quiet and abiding *communio* of hearts. You begin to experience the mystery of your own life as you increasingly allow the Holy Spirit to be the active agent, or the animator, of God's mission within you. You begin to experience and treasure the mystery of the perfection, ultimately, of all things as they, like you yourself, are moving to fullness in God, in Christ. You begin to notice a shift or a maturing in your encounter with God and with Jesus in prayer, moving from "praying for many things" to a more wordless indwelling in the Holy Trinity, at peace in the perfection of God's inscrutable plan.[95]

The third indicator of mature vocational awareness is a willingness to be *led by the Holy Spirit to look deeply within* to further discern God's calling. This work of following the lead of the Holy Spirit might be compared to following the sure and measured movement of the most exquisite dance partner.

---

[94] See Nemeck and Coombs, *Called by God,* esp. chaps. 9 and 10.

[95] This movement can be typified in the dynamic at work between Martha ("busy with many things") and Mary ("choosing the better part") (see Luke 10:38–42). Eventually we find the opportunity to move from Martha to Mary, especially as we surrender our physical capacities with age or infirmity. This "wordless indwelling" is expressed also in Psalm 131: "I do not busy myself with great matters, / with things too sublime for me. / Rather, I have stilled my soul, / hushed it like a weaned child" (vv. 1b–2a).

This looking deeply within leads to a maturing of your life's work as you engage in your life in its particular milieu in a more reflective, responsible way. Perhaps Jesus urged his disciples to "come away to a quiet place" precisely for this work of looking deeply within in order to be led more surely by the Holy Spirit.

The fourth indicator of mature vocational awareness is a *shift from reliance on others to a more intimate attentiveness to God dwelling within*. Here God becomes the soul's true director. For the more introverted person, reliance on others may never have been that appealing, and so this more intimate, interior attentiveness may not be something new. But for the extroverted person—and our culture is predominantly extroverted—this shift from reliance on others to that more intimate attentiveness to God may feel foreign. Processing the deeper, more interior workings of God's calling becomes less a "public" work and, over time, may become a work more suited to conversation with a few deeply trusted others.

At this point in your vocational journey you can expect deep interior shifts to occur; long-held hopes, beliefs, and commitments may begin to look different. You may actually begin to view your life's horizon with new vigor.

Obstacles to Vocational Discernment

David Whyte notes in his book, *Crossing the Unknown Sea: Work as a Pilgrimage of Identity,* that "we are the one part of creation that can refuse to be itself."[96] When I came across this passage I understood immediately what he was talking about. Not only working with others as a spiritual and vocational director but as a human being living my own life, I encounter the sad truth of this insight. I include myself in that human resistance to becoming fully an authentic self—the self whom God desires.

Clearly you *can* refuse to become your authentic self-in-God. But in

---

[96] David Whyte, *Crossing the Unknown Sea: Work as a Pilgrimage of Identity* (New York: Riverhead, 2001), 7.

doing so you not only steal from yourself your inheritance of joy, but you also steal from God the inestimable joy of communing with you in the divine banquet here and now. This refusal to become one's authentic self-in-God, I suspect, is what St. Paul meant when he cautioned against "grieving the Holy Spirit."[97]

Why is it that moving in God's direction can seem so difficult? I would like to focus on four common obstacles that can throw us off course.

The first obstacle to moving in God's direction is *clutter*. This can include the sea of *material* clutter—the sheer overflow of stuff, and the leaking away of time, energy, and resources in procuring stuff, storing stuff, arranging stuff, programming it, maintaining it, and all the effort it takes to work around your stuff, find it when it is lost, and finally, figuring out how to deprogram and recycle or otherwise dispose of your stuff when it is no longer useful to you. Then there is *activities* clutter—where you find yourself running in too many directions and always feeling just slightly off-balance, scattered, and spiritually off-center because you no longer find time to focus on what—or Whom—really matters.

Relational clutter occurs when you hold on to relationships that draw you away or distract you from your true center, which is your life in Christ. Relational clutter also occurs when you hold on to unforgiveness which deprives relationships of their rightful graced authenticity.

Finally, *spiritual* clutter, which can appear to be quite benign, or even a sign of holiness, is in fact insidious. Spiritual clutter includes the accumulation of habits and rituals and devotions and practices that can lull you into a numbed mediocrity and stunt your interior growth, or that may promise to give you what it cannot possibly deliver. Spiritual clutter keeps you from experiencing the interior simplicity that allows God to breathe in you and through you.

The second obstacle to moving in God's direction is an *underdeveloped*

---

[97] See Ephesians 4:30.

or irregular prayer life. These two are not the same. An *underdeveloped prayer life* can be described as lacking a *variety and depth* of personal prayer relative to your stage in life. It reveals an undeveloped capacity to meaningfully reflect on life circumstances or experience. When access to resources for your spiritual development end at, say, twelfth grade, the assumption can be that one has learned all one needs to know for the Christian spiritual life. As a result, spiritual literacy can lag far behind and cannot contribute to one's social-relational or professional literacy.

The *irregular prayer life* reflects a lack of *commitment* to regular prayer, oftentimes accompanied by a disinterest in the deep work of *liturgical* prayer within the Christian community. The person with an irregular prayer life may underestimate the importance of *accountability* to a confessor, spiritual director, or vocational guide. The man or woman of mature faith accepts that prayer is not something that you do when you can fit it into your schedule. In our results-driven culture, prayer—which produces nothing of tangible, bankable value—can seem like a waste of perfectly good time. For the person moving in God's direction, however, regular prayer and intimate relationship with God forms the *center* from which every dimension of one's life flows and to which every dimension of one's life returns.

The third obstacle to moving in God's direction is a *misshapen theology of vocation,* an obstacle which is not difficult to understand. Honest talk on the nature of God's calling must begin at the earliest stages of spiritual growth, and must be integral to the whole of catechesis in every stage of life. A robust and helpful theology of vocation must be encountered as a Gospel imperative for every baptized person, and not perceived as merely a calling for the few. The Christian community owes its members worthy resources to support discernment of God's calling in every stage of life. No aspect of child, youth, young adult, or mature adult catechesis should ever be separated from its vocational dimension. A robust theology of vocation speaks to the very purpose of human existence.[98]

The fourth obstacle to moving in God's direction, not surprisingly, is *sinfulness*. Specifically, this obstacle includes sinful actions, omissions, or habits; resistance to *moral formation* appropriate to your stage in life; resistance to *moral accountability;* and resistance to accepting responsibility for participation in the *social* dimensions of sin. In contemporary culture, "guilt" is a socially unacceptable word and responsibility for one's sinful actions can be passed off to forces and influences beyond oneself, or argued away by the right legal team. Many people struggle to come to grips with their role in broken relationships, broken institutions, broken systems of governance, and ultimately a broken world. Acknowledging one's sinfulness and taking active responsibility for the consequences of one's sin actually frees a person to participate in the Lord's own redemptive healing of the world, which essentially is a vocational work.

Experiencing obstacles in your work of maturing as a person and in your wholehearted engagement in life is part of the terrain you will encounter along your spiritual path. Honestly acknowledging and examining these obstacles and their impact on your vocational journey is necessary and worthy work in the context of spiritual and vocational direction. Appendix 3 offers seven steps in vocational discernment to guide your lifelong spiritual journey.

Next we will explore the role of mature prayer in the lifelong process of moving in God's direction.

---

[98] Awakening Vocations' four-workshop process of the same name provides parishes with a theologically sound and broad foundation for lifelong vocation discernment for individuals in every stage and state in life; see www.awakeningvocations.com/awakeningvocations.html.

Bringing It Home

1. In my own life, what if *"Hoc est enim Corpus meum"* ("This is my Body") really is "what it's all about"? How does my life—including engagement in my relationships, my work, and in the concerns of the world—bear that out?

2. How would I describe my vocational journey so far? At what points in my life have I heard God calling—or at least experienced a deep yearning for something more? How would I describe the discernment process around that journey?

3. What am I discerning of God's calling in my life now? What invitation appears on my horizon?

4. Does my need to be needed by others get in the way of my being available to God? Where am I in that discernment process?

Hold this Thought

> I am gaining skill and grace in
> moving in God's direction.

10

MORE PRAYER, LESS WORDS

Contours of a Mature Christ-centered Prayer Life

Some years ago I led a three-day Lenten retreat for a bishop and the clergy of his diocese. On the third day, in my final talk, the bishop raised his hand. Immediately I wondered if I had unknowingly spoken some falsehood, or worse, spent three days missing the point. "Yes, Bishop," I said.

All eyes in the circle turned to him. Silence filled the room as he took a long deep breath. "Can you speak to us of prayer?"

Ah, I thought, *can I speak to you of prayer ...*

In a matter of seconds—because that's all the time I had—I pulled my thoughts together, diving interiorly to the core of things. In a few brief sentences I described how I pray, and I paused. Then I found the words to say of prayer what I know to be most true: *We pray because Jesus is not yet finished praying to his Father.*

Again, silence filled the room. At that moment I had no other words to speak. And I had no idea whether what I had just said made sense to those who were listening.

The bishop then spoke in a tone of humble awakening: "You put us all to shame."

I took the bishop's words to mean: *Our understanding of prayer has just undergone a radical shift.*

At the heart of authentic Christian spiritual life is prayer. In fact, at the heart of human life itself, at the heart of human experience, is some primal form of prayer, the intimate communication—or *communion*—which gives truth to the claim that being-in-relationship lies at the heart of everything. Like the actual physical heart of any living being, the heart of the spiritual life is hidden from the eye, the mighty hidden engine that moves the interior life forward, keeping it vital and alive.

Christian prayer takes many forms, ranging from informal conversation with God and spontaneous praise or petition to the ritual communal prayer of liturgical worship. But we can describe the core of all Christian prayer as *relationship with God.* As with every meaningful human relationship, even more so with the divine: This relationship will change you. Being in relationship with God is the means by which you become your authentic self-in-God.

What Does Mature Prayer Look Like?

Most of us churn our way through successive stages of prayer, just as we churn our way through successive stages of life. Not possessing any map to our life which could show clear markers to tell us where we actually are on this convoluted journey, we often stumble into relationship with the Holy Spirit who, we discover, was quietly waiting all along to form us in the ways of prayer that "give light to our path."[99]

Early on we learn petitionary prayer, which Jesus urged his followers to pray. "Ask and it will be given to you," we hear Jesus say to his disciples (Matthew 7:7). In his final discourse, with perhaps a tone of frustration or urgency, Jesus says, "Until now you have not asked anything in my name; ask and you will receive, so that your joy may be complete" (John 16:24). Mature petitionary prayer becomes the disarmed expression of utter dependence on God's love and provision, bringing the soul to an honest encounter with its radical poverty before God. The caution here is that petitionary prayer also can degenerate into a list of insistent requests for life as we would like it to be.

As the soul matures, petitionary prayer on its own falls short of that fuller expression as the soul deepens in relationship with God. Nonetheless, the soul's yearning for deeper and more intimate—and therefore more "dangerous" —prayer can be met with an instinctive though not intentional pushback. In my spiritual direction practice I often encounter directees who say: "My prayer life was really opening and I felt so close to God, and all of a sudden it has dried up. I feel nothing at all, and I keep trying to capture what I felt before." The truth is that intimacy of any kind—and more so intimacy with God—requires a complete unguardedness of self before the other, and therefore such unguarded intimacy is dangerous. This deeper and more intimate expression of prayer places you at the threshold of vulnerability.

Spiritually intimate and therefore spiritually dangerous prayer is prayer, not of our own crafting, which urges us to reveal ourselves unguardedly and give ourselves unconditionally to God who is beyond our understanding, complete Mystery. We give ourselves to Whom we cannot really fathom, not counting the cost. Spiritually dangerous prayer is *kenotic* prayer, a loving participation in the complete self-emptying, or *kenosis,* of Jesus, most fully demonstrated in his peaceful submission to his arrest, torture, and execution. In our prayer, or as a result of our prayer, none of us anticipates such crushing treatment. But this intimate, loving, trusting, unguarded prayer does free us, as

---

[99] See Psalm 119:105.

Jesus was freed, for a generous outpouring of self for the good of others, according to our circumstances.[100]

When our more practical self pushes back from such radical self-offering, we can easily revert to a less self-involving petitionary prayer and become stuck in a swirling eddy of self-preservation. This kind of self-initiated petitionary prayer holds us back from that threshold of existential vulnerability, because often this reversionary type of prayer is shaped by an underlying fear that someone or some core dimension of life will be wrenched from us, that our lives will no longer be our own.

For the soul that continues to resist a deeper, more intimate, and therefore more dangerous expression of prayer, another stage of prayer can be the "jukebox" stage, where you insert your quarter, select the tune, press the button, and you hear what you want to hear. We all have been there at one time or another. And every one of us has probably gone through the "bargaining" stage of prayer as well. "Dear God, I'll do whatever you ask if you will just ..."

While each of us, at one point or another, churns through these many stages of prayer, God still abides. The Holy Spirit does not abandon us.

But an *ever-maturing relationship* is the key to authentic prayer. I do not mean here relationship with "the God of my understanding," but relationship with the living, hidden God whose proper name is Mystery and whose inner name is Love and All-Compassion and Mercy and Peace. Because this relationship exists at God's initiative, it is dynamic and evocative, inviting you to participate, unexplainably, in the most intimate aspects of divine life, thereby enabling you to become your authentic self-in-God.

What this understanding of prayer as God's initiative tells us is that mature prayer is vocational to the core. How you are doing in your prayer life is not just a check-in topic in the spiritual direction session but rather, a vital element of the larger conversation between director and directee. Here honesty

---

[100] Regarding kenosis, see Philippians 2:7–8: "Rather, he emptied himself, / taking the form of a slave, / coming in human likeness; / ... becoming obedient to death, / even death on a cross."

and humility shape the words that are exchanged, and a deep leaning into the Mystery of God sets the pace through deep listening.

The Vocational Dimension of Prayer

In simplest terms, mature prayer could be described as less "me" and more "You," less words and more presence, less certainty and more trust. In fact, mature prayer over time leads to the unexpected spiritual frontier experience of dynamic "real presence," where the two become one, the human radiating the divine, God incarnate once again, here and now, uniquely enfleshed in your life and time and circumstances.

The human marriage relationship in its most perfect expression of total self-giving becomes the mirror image of the human soul in communion with the completely self-giving God. The Christian mystics, as well as mystics of other traditions, have spoken through the ages of this direct and deeply engaging relationship of intimate communion of the human and the divine.

Jesus makes clear that this intimate relationship is not of our choosing but of God's choosing, carried out not at our initiative but at God's initiative. "The Father and I are one," Jesus says,[101] assuring us that the words he speaks are words that come from the very heart of his own Abba. When he tells his disciples, "It was not you who chose me, but I who chose you,"[102] he means for us to understand that we too have been initiated into intimate and everlasting communion in God by the pure grace of God's desiring.

Mature prayer, eventually, becomes the unavoidable yielding of self, of soul, of one's own willing, to God's irresistible, inescapable, and purifying love. Prayer, in essence, becomes the language of God's unqualified and generous calling, and your unqualified and generous response. Vocation cannot be

---

[101] John 10:30.

[102] John 15:16.

understood apart from a life of intimate, radically self-involving prayer. Because of this deeply formative role of prayer in the maturing of the soul, prayer holds a place of privilege in the director-directee relationship—not only as a topic of holy conversation but as a shared experience.

Prayer and Holiness

It is easy to think of prayer as "something I do," and holiness as "something I strive for" or "something I hope to achieve." This thinking, while not at all uncommon, misses the point. Therefore it is vital that directors and directees are clear on the deep dimensions of prayer which express the soul's being-in-God.

In fact we do pray, and we do strive for holiness. But none of this praying and striving, ultimately, is about us. We are *participants in* our prayer and in our striving for holiness, but we are not the initiator. Nor are we capable of bringing our prayer, nor our striving for holiness, to fulfillment. Prayer and holiness are both expressions of our relationship with God and the fruit of that relationship. Being human—and therefore possessing no real wealth of our own —we cannot give to God what God has not first given to us, including prayer.

As noted earlier, prayer eventually becomes the unavoidable yielding of self to God's irresistible, inescapable, and purifying love. But how shall we describe holiness? Holiness is a word we use to point to what we do not really understand: the inner life of God, the pure, inextinguishable fire of love which purifies, in order to make like itself all that it touches. Love as purifying fire may be an apt description, perhaps, of the purifying fires of purgatory, where all that is not-God is burned away. What is the result of such purification? Holiness now becomes a living thing, and the means by which we enter into unobstructed participation in the life of the Holy Trinity. As we enter through "the gates of holiness"[103] into the life of the Holy Trinity we become not consumed and lost

---

[103] See Psalm 118:19 (in *Christian Prayer,* 1963 Grail translation).

but most fully distinct as the unique self we are in God.

God's holiness in us is revealed in the works we do and in the heart and intent with which we do them. Hence Jesus' insistence in the Beatitudes on purity of heart, acts of mercy and meekness, and a life of nonviolence, and his equal insistence on apostolic works of compassion, as illustrated in the parable of the Last Judgment. The life of beatitude and compassion is at once the means to holiness, or means to a life lived in God, and the enfleshed expression and revelation of that holiness and that divine life. Holiness, like prayer, is an expression of relationship. In the Beatitudes Jesus urges us toward a life of perfect love, compassion, and mercy. Why? Because perfect love, compassion, and mercy form the very essence of the life of the Holy Trinity.

Prayer and striving for God's holiness in every dimension of one's life must form a core element of the conversation within spiritual and vocational direction. These two dimensions of Christian spiritual life—prayer and the striving for holiness—are vital to the maturing of self and to the generous living of one's calling. And each requires honest and humble accountability.

Prayer at the Center of Your Life

Every time I speak on the topic of prayer, invariably someone will comment: "What you say really rings true, but I am just too busy to pray." Even though this person in the audience may not be directly accountable to me, I do not accept that excuse and I will challenge it. To say "I am just too busy to pray" is like saying, "I am just too busy to breathe." It is like saying, "I have so far to travel I just don't have time to put gas in the tank." Granted, you can breathe while you are busy doing other things, but I know for certain that you will get nowhere on an empty tank. When you are "too busy to pray," either you need to slow down your life to a less violent, more manageable and graceful pace or, if you truly carry the weight of an unusual burden of concerns, then you are too busy to *not* pray.

Or, a person might say, "My whole life is a prayer." True. But these words can come perilously close to naïve self-deceit. When everything is special, nothing is special. Even Jesus urged his disciples to "come away to a quiet place" of intentional self-renewal.[104] He didn't have in mind a day at the spa, but rather, a time of necessary spiritual recentering.

Dorothy Day practiced a consistent discipline of prayer, including daily Eucharist, rosary, plus at least two hours a day in meditation on the Scriptures. When you consider the volume of her writing, plus the constant physical demands of tending to the endless needs of the poor, the marginalized, and the hopeless, you can rightly ask: How did she have time for such a regimen of prayer? She would probably look you straight in the eye and ask you: How can I undertake this life and *not* pray in these ways?[105]

Years ago I caught a portion of a television interview with Archbishop Desmond Tutu. And I recall him saying that on especially busy days of travel and speaking, he would rise earlier than usual to allow additional time for unrushed prayer, perhaps an extra hour or two. I took his words to heart and immediately adopted that practice, rising sometimes as early as 12:30 or 1:00 a.m. for unrushed prayer before leaving home for an early flight and a full weekend of teaching. What I have found, *every time without fail,* is that on those travel days, when I finish teaching at 9:00 p.m., I feel as refreshed as though I had enjoyed a full night's sleep.

None of us can excuse ourselves from the call to regular prayer that lies at the heart of a Christ-centered life and defines a mature relationship with God. Shifting the paradigm from prayer as "one more thing to do" to prayer as intentional expression of my being-in-God is important vocational work. Each of us is anointed to be a unique self-in-God before we are called upon to "do something," even if what we do is, in the words of Blessed Theresa of Calcutta, "something beautiful for God."

---

[104] See Mark 6:31.

[105] See Ellsberg, ed., *Dorothy Day,* xviii.

To help my directees to place prayer at the center of their life I ask them to imagine their life diagrammed as a wheel, a circular frame connected by spokes that unite at the hub. The "hub" is that place, within the self, of God's indwelling, the center that holds the many dimensions of one's life together. The hub allows the wheel to go around. The spaces between the spokes contain the various dimensions of one's life, such as prayer, study, work, family, other relationships, social concerns, hospitality, apostolic works, care for creation, self-care. They all have a place within the wheel, and all are part of what makes your life move forward, but they all find their place *in relation to the hub.*

Likewise, in the overall endeavor of your life, abiding with God at the center gives meaning and a rightful place to the many dimensions of your life. The effects of dwelling with God at the center flow outward and give shape and context and meaning to a life which is authentically yours.

Reciprocally, the circumstances and the commitments and concerns of your life flow back to the center, informing your indwelling in God with new levels of meaning and rich resonance.[106]

This circular and nonhierarchical model of life and prayer, where abiding in God at the center infuses every dimension of your life with vitality and meaning, is very different from a linear or "ladder" model where whatever is at the top—such as relationship with God—becomes increasingly distanced from meaningful conversation with those dimensions of your life that are "lower" on your list of commitments.

Your Prayer is not Your Own

"We are so poor," writes Johannes Metz in his classic essay *Poverty of Spirit*, "that even our poverty is not our own; it belongs to the mystery of

---

[106] Titled the "Vocation Wheel," this two-page model is available at www.awakeningvocations.com/welcome.html, under "Free Downloads."

God."[107] If not even our poverty belongs to us, then we know, by extension, that our prayer, which is an expression of our poverty, does not belong to us either.

In fact, St. Paul says as much: "For we do not know how to pray as we ought, but the Spirit itself intercedes" (Romans 8:26). This type of prayer to which St. Paul refers originates in God and ends in God. We find a qualitative and even viscerally measurable difference between a "please gimme" kind of prayer, the jukebox prayer, the bargaining prayer, and authentic prayer where "the Spirit itself intercedes." As your prayer matures and deepens you begin to physically feel the difference between self-initiated or self-directed prayer and prayer that flows from God, through you, and back to God. In self-initiated prayer we try, earnestly but mistakenly, to change God. In Spirit-initiated prayer *we* are changed. Through authentic prayer we find the means to become willing participants in God's work in us and God's work through us.

Your prayer is not your own, St. Paul rightly insists, because, being baptized and anointed in Christ, your *life* is not your own. It's not that your life has been hijacked by God. Rather, your life has been reclaimed for an unimaginably worthy purpose: to participate, with rightful dignity, in the work of revealing the reign of God at this time and place in human history, in the ways God has in mind.

This praying of the Holy Spirit in you may surprise you; it will take your prayer where you had not imagined, as the Spirit intercedes "with inexpressible groanings," as St. Paul writes. "And the one who searches hearts knows what is the intention of the Spirit, because it intercedes for the holy ones according to God's will" (Romans 8:27). Does this phrase "inexpressible groanings" mean that you will be praying in tongues? Many people do not have the gift of tongues, and yet they are men and women of profound and intimate prayer. At a spiritually difficult time in her life, Saint Thérèse of the Child Jesus complained to her spiritual director Père Pichon that all she had to give Jesus was just a sigh. He pointed out to her that a sigh has the power to move the heart of God. "Dare, then," Père Pichon admonished the saint, "to complain again at

---

[107] Metz, *Poverty of Spirit,* 51.

having only a sigh!"[108]

Indeed, your prayer is not your own. Along with every other dimension of your life, your prayer belongs to God. When your prayer feels constricted and overworded, or dry and elusive, allow yourself to come before God with nothing more than an honest sigh, or tears, and let it be enough, until more is given.

Contemplative Prayer

Many spiritual directors and many people who seek spiritual direction feel drawn to contemplative prayer. Why is this? Contemplative prayer, like spiritual direction, is about *listening to the innerness of things.* Like spiritual direction, contemplative prayer draws individuals into the deeper, more hidden but vital aspects of their life, and into loving dialogue with the One who not only dwells in the center of all things but *is* the center of all things. But what, really, is contemplative prayer? How shall we describe it?

This form of prayer can be different things to different people. There is no one textbook definition of "contemplative prayer," although enough models exist to give one a sense of the practice. Nor is contemplative prayer reserved for a few people with a monastic or mystical bent. Here are some descriptions and helpful insights from experienced practitioners of contemplative prayer to guide your own contemplative prayer practice.

John Main, OSB, speaks of "prayer of the heart," which he describes as a lifelong process of learning to pay attention to the Real Presence within self, others, and the world. This interior prayer is an indwelling, a silent *communio* in which we participate in the life of the Divine.[109]

---

[108] John Clark, OCD, trans., *Letters of St. Thérèse of Lisieux, Vol. II, 1890–1897* (Washington, DC: ICS, 1988), 767.

[109] Laurence Freeman, ed., *John Main: Essential Writings* (Maryknoll, NY: Orbis, 2002, 2004).

Henri Nouwen, in *The Way of the Heart*,[110] describes "hesychastic prayer," a form of prayer of the Eastern Orthodox church which takes seriously the words in St. Matthew's Gospel: "Go to your inner room, close the door, and pray to your Father in secret" (Matthew 6:6). This form of prayer, Nouwen notes, "leads to that rest where the soul can dwell with God." Hesychastic prayer, says Nouwen, provides entry into stillness of spirit, rest, quiet, and silence, a stilling of the senses in order to encounter God.

Thomas Keating, OCSO, founder of Contemplative Outreach, speaks of "centering prayer" which is "a method of silent prayer that prepares us to receive the gift of contemplative prayer, prayer in which we experience God's presence within us, closer than breathing, closer than thinking, closer than consciousness itself."[111] Keating notes that this form of prayer "is both relationship with God and a discipline to foster that relationship."

While many people are drawn to the study and practice of a particular method of contemplative prayer, such as those described above, others prefer the more immediate and interactive experience of sitting with Scripture, as in *lectio divina*. Here, ideally, a brief passage of Scripture is read *to* you, so that you can *receive* the spoken Word.[112] After a time of silence, which may be anywhere from a brief moment to an extended twenty or thirty minutes, you *receive* the Word as it is read a second time, and receive as gift the distinctive word or phrase or image that becomes for you the treasure, the pearl of great worth, embedded within the passage. After another extended period of silence the Word is heard and received a third time. This third reading, when delivered reverently and unrushed, is not heard as "repetition" but as a full and unexpected blossoming of the Word interiorly, where you experience an unexpected opening to a deeper understanding of the treasure you have received.

---

[110] Henri J. M. Nouwen, *The Way of the Heart: Desert Spirituality and Contemporary Ministry* (New York: HarperCollins, 1981).

[111] Thomas Keating, OCSO, Contemplative Outreach (www.centeringprayer.com/index.html, accessed January 20, 2012).

[112] Alternately, you can read the passage yourself. But there is a remarkable difference between *receiving* the Word that is spoken to you and decoding the words which you yourself read on a page.

All of these practices of contemplative prayer lend themselves to a group spiritual direction setting. Following the particular practice, gentle conversation can thread together a rich tapestry of spiritual insight of the group. Additionally, participants often receive insight, understanding, and a deeper appreciation for the trajectory of their own interior journey and the interior journey of others in such intimate communal encounters with the living Word of God.

Building a Habit of Prayer

Prayer never "just happens," any more than relationships of great value and meaning "just happen." Given the hectic and interruptive pace of life and the on-demand nature of contemporary culture, you can count on having to intentionally carve out time for prayer before the demands and distractions of the day can gain a foothold. In fact, building a habit of prayer is the surest way to guard against falling into the taken-as-normal vortex of craziness which is in fact a seductive form of lifestyle violence. Indeed, a well-protected habit of prayer is a prerequisite to a life of nonviolence and peacemaking and a strong, clear, and steadfast witness to the Gospel.

I cannot speak for those in monastic life whose days are shaped by the rhythms of communal prayer. But for Christian men and women in the world, prayer can often be perceived as an interruption, and therefore we can easily take prayer to be a bother. Especially for lay men and women who follow the cycle of psalms and prayer to mark the beginning, the middle, and the closing of the day, prayer clearly *interrupts* the customary flow of work and activities.

But prayer at set hours can be an interruption in a positive way, disrupting the flow and busy hum of the day in order to generate fresh spiritual capacity, the way a dam interrupts the flow of a river in order to generate energy. As Japanese Carmelite Augustine Ichiro Okumura observes, both of these interruptions—the dam on a river and the call to prayer—create energy: one electrical, the other spiritual.[113] Poet and author David Whyte writes of the hours of the day in the broad framework of this liturgical practice, and affirms these necessary interruptions that help us to transition toward a different rhythm of labor as the day progresses.[114]

Yet prayer, or this intentional turning toward God, is more than an interruption. It is holy conversation of the soul with God, much as spiritual direction is holy conversation between director and directee. The practice of prayer as conversation strives toward a certain rhythm of frequency until a habit of encounter with God in this way is firmly in place. In my own prayer practice I find that I must defend a space for prayer, especially in the noon hour, and at the close of the workday, since my workday can easily find no definite cut-off point. Defending that space of prayer is seldom easy. I would much rather stay with the flow of my work, but I also know that real refreshment and spiritual and mental renewal comes from regularly resting in God.

You can do certain simple things to ensure that prayer will occur regularly, so that its rhythm can support a wholehearted engagement in life. To build a habit of prayer, you must build the interior habit, or disposition, of dwelling in God. This does not mean escaping the world in order to sit in silence. The first work in building the habit of dwelling in God is to throw away the door of your heart—a radical work indeed, and not for the spiritually timid. When you throw away the door of your heart you make it unnecessary for God to even have to knock.[115] How do you actually throw away the door of your heart? Such work requires a generosity, an expansiveness of spirit, and a liberating trust in God. Here are four steps which you can repeat daily:

First, contemplate God everywhere, *everywhere,* especially in the difficult or even heart-crushing situations you would rather filter out. Second,

---

[113] Augustine Ichiro Okumura, OCD, *Awakening to Prayer* (trans. Theresa Kazue Hiraki and Albert Masaru Yamato) (Washington, DC: ICS, 1994), 58–59.

[114] Whyte, *Crossing the Unknown Sea,* chap. 10.

[115] This "throwing away the door of the heart" was the radical urging of John Paul II in his inaugural homily. See my essay, "Throw Open the Door of Your Heart" in *Touching the Reign of God,* 1–5.

bring everything to God, including the things you would rather hide. Third, give thanks for everything, even though you do not understand why these circumstances are now your lot in life, or the lot handed to others. And fourth, intentionally and daily seek *God's* desiring for your life and for the life of the world you inhabit.

As these practices of dwelling in God begin to take root in your life, you can begin to build an actual habit of prayer. How do you do this?

1. Create a place—no matter how small—that is for prayer only, and dedicate specific times to being in that space.

2. Regularly quiet yourself interiorly to practice a worshipful silence.

3. Learn your particular prayer language or "prayer vocabulary"— those few words or phrases that express your inmost self before God.

4. Pray without ceasing—not so much with words but with an interior orientation and disposition of heart, especially inspired by Scripture.

5. Pray for your adversaries; name them and pray earnestly for their good.

6. Pray in the variety of ways (including singing, postures, and gestures) that are authentic expressions of your inmost self before God.

7. Allow times and even seasons of spiritual dryness when God leads you on a pathless way; stay present to God during these times, and stay present to your life.

8. Intentionally set aside time to retreat, preferably on a regular basis (for example, quarterly).

Prayer that is strong enough and true enough to sustain you through life never "just happens." As with any worthwhile relationship, prayer as *communio* in God seeks to be nurtured; and as with any helpful habit, such prayer needs to be practiced with intention and care. That is why we refer to these ways of prayer as prayer *practices*. They do not happen on their own. They require your wholehearted and loving care. Spiritual and vocational directors should be willing to share with their directees the prayer practices that sustain them, and speak competently of the variety of prayer practices that shape their own inner life.

Bringing It Home

1. Why do I pray? What actual reasons can I list that explain *why* I pray?

2. How has my prayer changed over the past few years? How has my prayer changed in the past six months? What has precipitated or guided these changes?

3. How has my prayer led to clarity about how God is calling me at this time in my life, or how God was calling me at some early point in my life?

Hold this Thought

Through prayer I am experiencing the refreshment and strength of soul

that comes from dwelling in God.

11

INTEGRATING GOD'S MOVEMENT

Finding Freedom of Speech in the Direction Session

"Speak," the young Samuel says when he finally understands that the Lord God is desiring to draw the lad into a relationship of prophetic service. "Speak, LORD, for your servant is listening."[116]

Your servant is listening. Interestingly, Samuel does not say, "If you speak, I will listen." No, he says, in essence, "I am listening. I have placed myself in a posture of readiness to hear you, to receive your words and to act on them." This attitude and even physical posture of openness to hearing what the Lord God has to say describes the very core of the word *obedience,* which means *to listen with the ear of the heart,* and to act accordingly. This attitude and orientation of the interior self toward listening lies at the heart of spiritual and vocational direction. This conversation is indeed privileged and holy conversation: The director listening to the directee, the directee listening to the

---

[116] For the full story of the call of the young prophet Samuel, see 1 Samuel 3:1–10.

emerging words of conversation, and both listening together, in the words and in the silent spaces, to "the still small voice" of the Holy Spirit.[117]

Four Kinds of Speech

In the course of all this listening, both director and directee often begin to discover that not all speech is the same. I have come to identify four kinds of speech which emerge not only in the course of spiritual and vocational direction but in the flow of daily discourse.[118] These four kinds of speech offer a glimpse into the quality of one's interior conversation and the overall freedom—or lack of freedom—which one is experiencing at this point in one's life. For authentic and fruitful direction to occur, both director and directee must become aware not only of the type of speech that is being used, but what that type of speech is communicating "between the lines." These four types of speech include *spiritually empty speech, spiritually false* speech, *spiritually unfree* speech, and *spiritually free* speech. We will look at each one in turn.

1. *Spiritually empty speech* is the ongoing mindless chatter, both verbal and electronic, that fills every pocket of silence in our world today. Whether I am sitting in a church attempting to ready my soul in silence as people gather for worship, or whether I am standing in line at the supermarket or at a crowded gate at the airport, I am hemmed in by endless chatter about things that will be irrelevant and forgotten in twenty minutes. Empty speech communicates precious little of meaning or substance. More often it serves as a constant interruption of any attempt toward focused deeper thought, an interruption that seems benign enough, but eventually becomes spiritually corrosive. Why? Spiritually empty speech keeps not just individuals but entire populations within our contemporary global culture distracted from being intentionally and wholeheartedly present to things that matter.

---

[117] See 1 Kings 19:12.

[118] The ideas expressed here originally appeared in my article, "Listening the Other Into Free Speech," *Presence,* 14:1 (March 2008), 29–33.

2. *Spiritually false speech* is speech that reveals a jarring disconnection between a person's interior self and outer response to undesired or challenging circumstances. It is treasonous speech, betraying the reality of a person's inner experience. Spiritually false speech dismisses the deeper reality of the circumstances of life and blocks honest acknowledgment of the deeper truth of one's personhood. Statements such as the following should alert the attentive spiritual director that an unspoken anguish needs to be addressed.

"I've got to be strong," the directee with stage four cancer might say, whose family is wrestling with layers of dysfunction and denial. What this person actually, though unconsciously, might be asking of the director is permission to fall apart in order to undergo the deep spiritual work of dying and entry into the next stage of life.

"It probably is not that big a deal," a directee might say when describing the loss of something that has been meaningful, or when someone else has offended or ignored or unjustly taken credit for what the directee has done. The mistaken belief that such a directee may be telegraphing to the director is: "This experience probably does not matter that much to God, and so it shouldn't matter to me. But it does. But it hurts so much that I cannot admit it." By extension the directee unknowingly may be saying: "I do not believe (or no longer believe) that my life or my experience matters all that much in the eyes of God."

"I guess this is what I'm supposed to settle for" is another phrase that reveals spiritually false speech, either in words or in embodied attitude. This may be the message of the directee who has been betrayed in a relationship that never did find solid grounding. It often is the phrase expressed by people who feel locked into a marriage or a job or even a deeply invested career that never did have their name on it. This tone of resignation can sometimes be heard in the single person who seems unable to "find a mate" and who has no words and no way to discern a positive calling to celibate life. Spiritually false speech simply swallows—unchewed, so to speak—an individual's bitter encounter with disappointment, injustice, or loss of hope. It reveals an incapacity to probe

beyond face value for the deeper connective meanings that make sense of a complex yet worthy life.

3. *Spiritually unfree speech* is the most anguished of these types of speech, and verbalizes the emotional pushback that can encage and shackle a person for years, or even decades. Spiritually unfree speech reveals the prolonged, profound pain of one's spiritual and emotional unfreedom, often revealing victimhood long trapped in blame and unabated anger, or a heart resistant to divine grace.

"I refuse," "I can't," "I will never" often are expressions of spiritually unfree speech. Such phrases communicate that the door of the heart is closed to reconsideration or to a shift of perspective. At funerals it is not unusual to see gray-haired siblings or the middle aged son or daughter of the deceased sit with arms crossed, unmoved and determined to not be touched—and therefore rendered vulnerable—by the loss of *this* life, the closing of *this* chapter, and the challenge of forgiveness and the healing of relationship.

Spiritually unfree speech leaves little room for God's movement, yet often rails against God for abandoning the soul in turmoil. Spiritually unfree speech reveals a soul's encounter with terrifying discouragement. In its more entrenched state spiritually unfree speech exposes the toxins of spiritual infection and a cry for healing. For the director the challenge here is not to helpfully coax the directee into a place of openness to interior vulnerability. Rather, the real challenge is to gently and reverently *walk with* the directee through the layers of stuckness, toxic emotional muck, resistance, and actual pushback; then, in the dark, most hidden and broken place, to find, at last, the unexpected reason for hope and graced possibility.

This unexpected reason for hope is the light which St. Paul says "shines out of darkness."[119] Continuing his metaphor, insight and spiritual liberation come when the directee assents to become the cracked and fragile earthen vessel

---

[119] See 2 Corinthians 4:6.

through which the light of Christ irrepressibly shines.[120] For the director this work requires complete givenness to patience, reverence, genuine love of the directee, and the fine-tuned guidance of the Holy Spirit.

4. *Spiritually free speech,* quite the opposite of unfree speech, reveals something of the authentic self-in-God, and gives, or at least strives to give, worthy language to the complexity and mystery of the directee's circumstances in life. The starting point of spiritually free speech is the deep understanding: *I am beloved of God.* This living reality governs and shapes the words, attitudes, and actions of the spiritually free person. Spiritually free speech flows from a living relationship with one's own interior self and with God, a living relationship which gives context and meaning to all of one's other relationships and to one's life circumstances. The focus of spiritually free speech is not "perfection" but openness to God and to engagement in the divine Mystery in the circumstances of one's life.

The directee who engages in spiritually free speech may say, in essence: *"This is my experience, and this is how I am reflecting on it"* when working on an emotionally or morally perplexing situation or unwelcome shift in circumstances. The directee who engages in spiritually free speech expresses an active engagement in difficult or unanticipated situations, sensing a work of the Holy Spirit, and is content to abide in God in the "place of unknowing." In the presence of the director's deep listening, the spiritually free directee can speak the *incongruence* between one's poverties and God's love, between one's sinfulness and God's mercy, between one's small-heartedness and God's persistent generosity. In the midst of spiritual paradox, spiritually free speech reveals something of the directee's interior centeredness in God. Spiritually free speech reflects the directee's capacity to enter into the arduous work of dying and receiving new life which lies at the heart of the paschal mystery and dynamic life in Christ.

---

[120] See 2 Corinthians 4:7.

Spiritually Free Speech and the Maturing Self

These four categories of speech apply as much to the director as they do to the directee. The deeply healing and integrative work of spiritual and vocational direction depends in great measure on the quality of speech of both director and directee. Spiritually free speech both evokes and reveals the maturing self-in-God, whether that be the self of the director or the self of the directee. The dedicated spiritual director is also a directee, speaking to another "trusted other" from an interior place of honesty, and receiving the deep listening and wise guidance which fosters insight. The holy work of spiritual direction is to listen the other into a place of interior freedom, to actually listen the other into authentic personhood.

The effects of being listened into interior freedom are fourfold, suggest Nemeck and Coombs.[121] A *first effect* of spiritually free speech is the ability to enter into what the authors describe as *self-intimacy,* the ability to listen honestly and patiently to yourself in all the facets of your life. This quality of listening interiorly enables you to enter into mature and dynamic relationship with others and to engage in creative interaction with your world.

A *second effect* of spiritually free speech is the ability to *lovingly embrace your uniqueness.* Far from capitulating to the "I am special" attitude so prevalent in contemporary American culture, embracing the uniqueness of your personhood exposes you to not only the grace but also the poverty of the uniqueness of your being, as Metz poignantly describes.[122] Listening the directee into the freedom to honestly acknowledge God-given goodness, beauty, and truth opens the directee to a fresh experience of self-worth and anointing for a worthy purpose in the reign of God.

A *third effect* of spiritually free speech is a *freedom to listen to the other.* Such selfless, generous listening becomes an act of love. Here one is free to set aside personal interest and the need to be heard in order to encounter and

---

[121] See Nemeck and Coombs, *The Way of Spiritual Direction,* esp. 56–66.

[122] See Metz, *Poverty of Spirit,* 38–39.

receive the gift of the other's being, circumstances, and otherness. Generally, those who are more introverted may more easily express this freedom to listen to the other, simply because they are less inclined to process their own experiences with others outside a trusted circle.

A *fourth effect* of spiritually free speech is a *deeper capacity to listen to God.* This, ultimately, is the desired fruit of spiritual and vocational direction: Not only director listening to directee, and directee listening with ever-growing freedom to director, but *the two, together, listening to God.*

Taken together, these four effects of spiritually free speech enable the directee to move willingly, wholeheartedly, and gracefully in God's direction. This deep interior freedom is not merely for those who feel moved to seek it out. This maturing of self through the freedom to speak one's truth honestly, and the freedom to be heard and understood, is a deep-seated *human* longing, and is absolutely necessary to sustain meaningful and worthy relations between individuals, within and among cultures and societies, and between humankind and all of creation.

Even our enemies have a truth to speak, carrying, perhaps, wounds that are not unlike our own. Our polluted air, crumbling hillsides, choked streams, and fracked substrata also have a truth to speak, and deserve to be listened to, heard, and understood. This urging toward deep interior freedom is as necessary as air and the capacity to breathe it, as essential as food and the ability to draw nourishment from it. Such freedom is our human birthright, bestowing on each of us the dignity of our being made in the image of God.

Practical Ways to Call Forth Spiritually Free Speech

Spiritual directors undertake a twofold task as they minister to others through the holy work of listening. The *first task,* not confined to the direction session, applies to the whole of the director's life. Specifically, this task is the work of listening humbly and intentionally to the director's own speech—to the interior conversations and the conversations one has with the world. The spiritual director who has not yet become quieted of the noise of empty speech, or whose phrases are laced with false speech, or who bears the burden of unfree speech, is not yet entirely free to enter into the spiritually and emotionally delicate work of discerning the spiritual authenticity of the speech of another.

Our contemporary culture seems to thrive on a "reality" style of reaction to circumstances. We seem predisposed to sharing the mundane, the intimate, and the unprocessed experiences of life in a barrage of spontaneous, unfiltered "tweets." To counter this chaos, today's spiritual director must intentionally take a quieter, less dramatic, more modest, and more authentic approach to the speech of self-expression. The vigilant director could well take to heart the words of the Psalmist: "Set, O LORD, a guard over my mouth; / keep watch at the door of my lips."[123]

The *second task* of spiritual directors as they minister to others in the holy work of listening now becomes easier and more beneficial: to listen with a cleansed inner spirit and a fine-tuned ear to the verbal language—the word choice, the tone, the phrasing of the directee's language; and to the more subtle language of "presence"—posture, gestures, facial expression—which directees use to express their inner life.

These disciplines of deeper listening build upon a director's ability to engage in and sustain such other-focused listening in a way that sets the directee free to say precisely all that needs to be said. Personality, too, brings much to bear on the quality of deep listening that is solely focused on the other. The director with a more introverted personality is more likely to be comfortable "learning about you" than "talking about me." As noted earlier, extroversion does not disqualify one from being a deeply listening spiritual director, but it more likely will require a greater degree of discipline on the part of the extroverted director in the communication dynamic within the relationship.

How can the spiritual and vocational director build capacity to call

---

[123] Psalm 141:3 (in *Christian Prayer,* 1963 Grail translation).

forth spiritually free speech in the directee? Here are five indicators that indicate that capacity.

1. Listening that evokes spiritually free speech in the other *does not interrupt.* The director refrains from judgment phrases such as "Oh, that's good," or "I'm glad to hear that," or "How terrible"—responses that merely tell the directee what you do or do not want to hear in future conversations. Even empathy, as we noted in chapter 2, must submit to the humble, noninterruptive work of other-centered listening.

2. Listening that evokes spiritually free speech *waits on what the Holy Spirit desires to be said.* Listening to the directee is only a portion of a director's work. Listening interiorly to the directee *and* to the still, small voice of the Holy Spirit is the real work—listening *through* the words of the other, *through* the presence and heart of the other, and *through* one's own heart and Spirit-guided intuition.

3. Listening that evokes spiritually free speech continually *seeks the deeper reality* of the directee's experience. "What was that like for you?" is not merely a question in search of detail, but a key that unlocks doors to the directee's perceptions and feelings around a circumstance. The question, "What was that like for you?" gently offers the directee permission to explore, own, and integrate a circumstance or experience into the complexity and mystery of personhood—specifically, the directee's personhood-in-God.

4. Listening that evokes spiritually free speech *moves the directee toward mature faith* and the work of discovering, embracing, and integrating God's movement in the circumstances of life. That our lives rightfully should produce the fruit of mature faith comes as a revelation to many. Yet producing the fruit of mature faith is a vocational imperative. Spiritual and vocational direction offers capacity for director and directee both to "produce good fruit" within their respective endeavors for the reign of God.

5. Finally, listening that evokes spiritually free speech *invites the other into creative participation* in God's redeeming activity in the world. This is the

outward movement that results from worthwhile inner work. Through the skilled, compassionate, and challenging work of spiritual and vocational direction, one by one men and women of deep Christian faith grow in their anointing to be the presence of the risen Lord in a complex twenty-first century world. This experience of holy listening clearly is the deeply vocational and spiritually evocative, invitational, and necessary work of such anointing.

The Art of Theological Reflection

One of the best kept secrets of adult faith development in the church today is the art and practice of theological reflection. Based on my observations as I speak in parishes across the nation, most men and women who are active in their faith have not heard the term "theological reflection" nor have they been introduced to the process of this discipline. Learning *about* the faith and studying the pillars of doctrine and belief and practice is typically the backbone of catechesis for adults, youth, and children. And living a moral and generous life is the ideal to which we aspire.

But the key—too often missing—which enables the forward movement of a well-expressed, fruitful and living faith is the *integrative* piece. The teachings of the church can be quite clear, but life often is experienced subjectively, more in nuanced shades, than objectively in crisp black and white. Our lived experience—whether we perceive it to be in black and white or in those nuanced shades—is not exempt from either the wisdom of the church nor the ongoing dynamic of paschal mystery—that hidden work of dying and receiving new life.

In simplest terms, theological reflection is the *imaginative and disciplined examination of your experience in light of the fullness of the Christian tradition.* It is a genuine, Spirit-guided dialogue between your beliefs, actions, and values, and the tenets and values of the church's sacred heritage. Theological reflection is not about tidying up the reality of your experience to meet the demands of the church's moral teaching, nor is it about bending such moral teaching to accommodate your experience. The point of reflecting theologically on your experience is to gain the insight, wisdom, and pastoral care of the church, and to undergo conversion as an expected and ongoing expression of a maturing faith. The dynamic of theological reflection seeks the wisdom behind the teaching, as well as the wisdom embedded in human experience, in order to set you free to grow into your authentic self-in-God.

The *art* of spiritual direction is the skilled and imaginative interplay between self and the Holy Spirit, between circumstance and possibility, between the way things are and divine invitation, between givenness and grace. The imagination—namely, the anointed imagination, the Christian imagination—plays an enormous role in theological reflection. By *imagination* I do not mean fantasy or something imaginary or make-believe. Rather, the word points to that deeper work of seeking in one's life and one's soul the *image of God,* the particular image of God which evokes the deep mystery of one's unique and particular being.

Generally speaking, "art" refers to skill, craftsmanship, and the capacity to fashion something lovely or useful from ordinary—or sometimes discarded—material. So the art of theological reflection is that well-practiced ability to skillfully, honestly, imaginatively, and readily fashion what is new, redeemed, and life-giving from stuck or broken circumstances or from discarded though important memories from one's past.

A directee may share with me all the trauma of events in recent weeks. I listen, but I am not really listening for details of the trauma. I am listening for what the directee does with the harrowing experience, the anxious situation, or the lost opportunity, and how the directee partners with the Holy Spirit in the imaginative interplay between self, circumstance, and the wisdom and grace of the experience. It is this artful and imaginative interplay that brings power and unexpected positive outcome to the practice of theological reflection. The discipline of theological reflection requires you to be present to and actively engaged in your life, engaged in dynamic conversation with your circumstances and the foundations of a living faith that is strong enough to sustain you. This discipline requires you to be in active, intentional partnership with the Holy Spirit as your life's meaning becomes more fully revealed, especially in the perplexing circumstances and moral challenges that are unavoidable in the living of a human life.

The fruit of such Spirit-guided reflection, first of all, is a hope you can live with, even in the midst of interior brokenness and loss, a hope that can set you free despite the evidence. A further fruit of theological reflection is a more wholehearted and generous giving of self to God's willing. As you mature, that giving of self to God is not only for your own good, but for the good of others, and for the good of the world you touch. The quality of your reflection on your life matters because the choices you make, from the mundane to the moral, will impact others for good or for ill, now or in the future. Theological reflection on your life helps you to befriend your Christian heritage in a diverse and complex world, and to befriend your limited and imperfect life in the light of unbidden grace.

The Science of Theological Reflection

If the practice of theological reflection is a spiritual art, it also is a science—although it is not rocket science. Theological reflection is a reflective practice with a structure, a dynamic, and a processing of inputs that leads to an output. It is a process designed to move you more clearly in God's direction.

A helpful model[124] of how we experience life through the lens of theological reflection can be expressed in the following cycle:

Step 1: *Experience,* which leads to …

Step 2: *Feelings,* which lead to …

Step 3: *Interpretive images,* which lead to …

[124] I am indebted to the work of Killen and de Beer in *The Art of Theological Reflection,* esp. chap. 2.

Step 4: *Insight,* which leads to ...

Step 5: *Action,* which leads back to ...

Step 1: *More experience,* and so on.

Let's examine each of these elements in this cycle of theological reflection.

Step 1: *What life experience do I want to examine?* What situation or circumstance do I want to bring into conversation with Scripture and my Christian heritage and the fullness of the Christian tradition? In one sentence—or two at the most—how do I describe it? In *experience,* which is the practical starting point for the reflection process, the key element is *noticing,* developing the intentional practice of being aware of the contours and complexities of circumstances in the moment. Let us take, for example, a situation where, say, your neighbor's feral cat daily prowls around in your yard, hides in your bushes, and leaps out to capture and eat your unsuspecting backyard birds. Key questions that sharpen your capacity to notice are: *Who? What? When? Where? How?* These are simply journalistic data-gathering questions. But do not be tempted at this point to ask the question: *Why?* At this initial point you are simply gathering data.

Step 2: *How can I describe that experience in a way that gets me to the real heart of the matter?* What is this situation *really* about—for me? What are *my* issues—not the other person's issues—that need to be addressed? With *feelings,* which is the second step in the reflection process, the key element is the intentional practice of *joining body and mind in the search for meaning*—getting your gut involved. For some people, this physical embodiment of feeling comes easily. Yet a vast percentage of people in our culture experience a disconnection between head and heart, and lack a mature capacity to open themselves to honest feelings about their own very real and complex life experience. An honest expression of emotion, for many people, easily becomes an act of irrationality. Prescription drugs and various forms of self-medication have long provided a buffer from the difficult work of developing the powerful and therefore frightening feeling-self. The key question here is: *What questions, values, or wisdom do my feelings carry?* Anger, for example, is a messenger, an indicator, pointing the way to an interior work that needs to be done. Returning to our cat-eats-birds example, as you stand at your window and watch the neighbor's cat eviscerate yet one more of your chickadees, you feel a wave of rage wash through you, along with feeling a sudden, blinding urge to throttle the cat. But the damage is done, and the warm tasty tidbit is nearly devoured. It is important to name these feelings—not suppress them or magnify them, but *name* them—if you want to receive the gifts of honest insight embedded within them.

Step 3: *What part of the fullness of the Christian tradition speaks to the heart of the matter as I have named it?* What Scriptures, church teachings, or deeper realities of liturgical and sacramental living speak to the situation? And what are they saying? Allow ample time for this part of the interior dialogue. It may take weeks or longer for the full content of this conversation to be expressed. With *interpretive images,* the key element is *receiving the image-symbol* that relieves the weight of feeling. The overarching Christian image-symbol for human experience is the cross and resurrection—the paradox of dying in order to receive new life. This image-symbol of dying and receiving new life resonates throughout all of creation and through every dimension of human experience. The key question here is: *What image embodies or captures, carries or expresses, the feelings that arise from my experience?* As you name your rage and the urge to throttle the cat, you begin to realize: This is what cats do. Cats, feral to the bone, eat birds. This cat is doing what is in its nature to do.

Step 4: *From this conversation, what new insight, wisdom, truth, or meaning emerges for me?* What's the *aha* moment? What weight seems to be relieved? What unexpected wisdom or insight do I discover embedded in the church's heritage to help me here? What grace or interior liberation do I experience in my circumstance? With *insight,* the key element is *movement toward theological reflection.* Insight offers the *aha* moment, the small bright moment when God's hand becomes clear, oftentimes in the least expected way. The key question is: *What invitation from God lies in this experience, these feelings, this image?* None of us creates our own insights; we receive them as gifts. The invitation to insight will continue to be issued until we respond to it—

wholeheartedly, and with grace. The invitation here is to accept this small, hidden work of dying to self in the face of what feels like an injustice—the invasion of the neighbor's cat into your kingdom, your personal realm, your bird sanctuary. You begin to realize that, apart from the death of one more chickadee, your own work of dying is about letting go of what you cannot control. Weep, yes, perhaps, and let go.

Step 5: *Given this interior liberation, how might God be calling me to act or to be present to others in a new way?* How am I being challenged or invited to grow? How does this moral or spiritual insight set me free and impel me toward more responsible engagement in my world? In *action,* the key element is *incarnating God's willing,* and embodying God's love and compassion in the world. This is not about heroics, nor about claiming the self-righteous high moral ground. Rather, incarnation—giving flesh to God's willing —is about faithfulness and a joyful obedience that flows in these circumstances from a willing heart. The key question here is: *How is Christ more present in the world because of my experience and the growth, conversion, and liberation of my heart which flows by grace from that experience?* None of us takes action on our own; in every initiative that is for the good, we are led by the Holy Spirit to move in God's direction. So the action in our example is pretty clear. You know that you do not really want to physically harm the cat. Nor can you adequately seal off your yard from this invader and protect these wild birds from the ravages of nature's larger workings. Nor can you honestly shrug, at this point, and say this neighbor's-cat-eating-my-birds situation does not really matter. It does. The one option open to you is the one option you least want to face— another dying to self. You determine to fashion a conversation with your neighbor which gives the two of you the space to respectfully see the situation from each other's perspective, and then lean into the Holy Spirit for the right words, the helpful insights, a real conversation that actually enables each of you to experience your better selves and to engage the larger forces of reconciliation and peace. That is one expression of the true and hard-won fruit of theological reflection.

The Practice of Theological Reflection

Both directors and directees at least intuitively understand that, on our own, we oftentimes cannot fully trust our insights into why our lives are the way they are. Our insights are, well, *our* insights; by nature we feel partial to them. We are subjective insiders to our own experience. And both spiritual directors and directees begin to discover the good news embedded in this very subjective human limitation: None of us has to figure out the mystery of our lives *on our own*. This is the grace of spiritual and vocational direction.

That said, the connection between your lived experience and the church's wisdom may not always be clear—or convenient. Movement from intense feeling or spontaneous opinion to honest, intentional, soul-searching dialogue can be wrenching and slow, and it is always conversional. But it is a necessary dialogue nonetheless for the arduous journey toward mature Christian faith. Where do you start, or where do you even find the courage to start, this intentional and utterly honest dialogue that promises to change you?

Start where you are right now. You do not have to spiritually "pretty up" to become a worthy partner in this dialogue between your interior self and the Holy Spirit. In fact, to do so would rob you of authenticity and deny your reflection its capacity for deeper insight. To even try to tidy up your experience would render this process of reflection incapable of leading you to the sure movement of the Holy Spirit in the circumstances of your life.

Elements of this intentional dialogue between your interior self and the larger body of wisdom that can lead you to worthy theological reflection include:

1. Your *lived experience*—unadorned and honestly named;
2. The *church's tradition* which shapes or has shaped your life;
3. The *culture* which also shapes your life; and
4. Your *opinions* and your most *deeply held convictions*.

It is these last elements—your opinions and convictions—that can bring the greatest pushback in the challenging work of moral and spiritual growth. Our opinions and convictions form our statements of meaning, revealing our understanding of life. They can blind us to God's activity, or they can reveal, with unexpected clarity, that hidden activity already at work in our lives. Willingness to loosen our grip on, or even let go, our opinions and convictions gives the Holy Spirit room to move and lead the interior self to expressions of mature Christian faith.

This work of theological reflection is necessary work for both directors and directees. No one who is baptized is exempt from personal responsibility for this ever-maturing relationship with God. Likewise, each of us is personally responsible for an ever-maturing relationship with the church and an ever-deepening Christ-centered moral and social engagement in the concerns of our society, of our culture, and of the world.

You may find it helpful to reflect on your experiences by prayerfully sitting with the daily Lectionary readings.[125] Make use of this preeminent treasure of the church. The habit of turning daily to the Scriptures brings you into immediate conversation with the heart of the church's wisdom, offering you both moral challenge and spiritual consolation. Bring the fruits of this deeper engagement in Scripture to the holy conversation of spiritual direction.

---

[125] I recommend the Lectionary here over the entire Bible for three reasons: First, with the Lectionary, the readings are given; you don't have to "search" for the reading that *you* think will best speak to your situation. Second, turning occasionally to the Lectionary invites you to turn regularly to the Lectionary for daily spiritual nourishment. Third, humbly accepting the church's Scripture reading for the day stretches you spiritually and spares you the temptation to default to your "favorite" passages or to those passages that are sure to heap upon you the guilt you are convinced you deserve. Daily Lectionary readings can be found on numerous Web sites, and often are listed in the weekly church bulletin.

Bringing It Home

1. What do I talk about in my "self talk"? Would I describe it as sometimes empty speech? Sometimes dismissive false speech? Is my self-talk sometimes spiritually unfree speech revealing resistance or pushback? Could I describe my self-talk as spiritually free speech? What recent specific examples of self-talk come to mind?

2. Regarding my conversations with the people closest to me, either by choice or by circumstance, how would I describe the quality of my speech? With whom do I engage in empty chatter? With whom do I speak in dismissive tones? To whom do I speak angry words or spiritually unfree speech? With whom can I engage in spiritually free speech?

3. What do these various conversations and types of speech—interior as well as with others—tell me in helpful ways about myself?

Hold this Thought

I am becoming more mindful of the effects of my speech

on my interior life and on my spiritual growth.

12

LIVING IN GOD'S ECONOMY

The Well-Directed Home Life

Oftentimes in our eagerness to grow in the spiritual life we overlook, or even unknowingly discount, the spiritual dimensions of home life. However, the very mundane, day-to-day decision making of which chores we will do, and which chores we will put off, which purchases we will make, and which we will refrain from making, and all the criteria we employ in all of these choices become worthy matter for the holy conversation of spiritual direction. Why? Because even our mundane, day-to-day choices are moral choices, expressions of stewardship, expressions of what we value, what we support, or what we deem unworthy of our time, our resources, and our spiritual energy.

In the course of spiritual and vocational direction you can begin to appreciate more deeply that *how* you manage your household matters greatly for those within the household and for those whose lives they touch. How you spend your money, or apportion your household budget, impacts not only members of your household but members of the broader community, and impacts equally the integrity of the natural environment. How you care for the needs of others when times are tough within your own household reveals your understanding of the social dimensions of the Gospel. Everything—from your calendar and how you spend your time, to your credit card statements and how you spend your money —declares your moral priorities. All of this is worthy material for spiritual and vocational direction.[126]

Economic Recovery and the Reign of God

Every day we hear endless anxious chatter about "economic recovery." Reporters, pundits, and forecasters seem to micromanage every ounce of data they can squeeze out of corporate moves, claims for unemployment benefits, and consumers' spending. Economic "recovery" is a troubling phrase at best. Banks collapse. But then they reopen on Monday morning, propped up by funds not their own. Claims for unemployment benefits dropped last month. But oops, they're back up again. Homes fall into foreclosure, but maybe there's hope. Or maybe not. The winds of change blow in all directions at once.

What went wrong? How did we get to this state of constant financial chaos? From some economists' viewpoint, economic systems could no longer handle the strain of consumers' runaway spending. Others point out that when jobs go elsewhere, the unemployed are left behind to fend for themselves. Still others claim that social safety nets, commonly known as "entitlement programs," have hurled us into deficit spending.

More to the point, where did *we* go wrong? Economic systems do not crumble on their own. For some people within our culture, purchasing "the American dream" has come easily. However, for far too many people that American dream has been purchased at great human cost—first of all, the cost of life lived off balance, where the appetite for more drives our need to press harder for the means to pay for it all. We have become a nation of shoppers, a nation of

---

[126] Ideas presented here are expanded in my *Living in God's Economy: A Practical Guide for Christ-centered Households in Tough Economic Times* (Eugene, OR: Awakening Vocations, 2009.

"stuff junkies," restless for the next fix. And there's more human cost—just ask those here and abroad who work for low wages, often under unsafe conditions, unable to afford decent housing or adequate healthcare for their families, who produce low-cost goods to feed our insatiable American appetite for more great stuff at a really cheap price.

We sadly believe that robust consumer spending makes our nation strong. Instead, it has made us fat—perhaps in body, and surely in soul. We have become morally blinded to the diminished dignity and worth of those who become trampled in our stampede for more. And our biblically mandated stewardship of the commons—this one planet which we share—has become a relentless extraction of resources for personal convenience and corporate gain.

We live in a complex world that is out of control in its raging appetites, a world equally out of touch with its original grace, and beauty, and purpose. We have lost the rightly ordered relationship between self, God, neighbor, and the natural world which sustains us. In essence, our twenty-first century world is a system severely out of balance. Overstimulated and accustomed to a supersized lifestyle, we seem truly incapable of getting down to the sobering realities which could bring us back to center. We lack the discipline for meaningful conversation around questions that matter, questions like: How *do* we, and *will* we, reel in our runaway appetites so that God's goodness and life's necessities are available to everyone? How *do* we, and *will* we, move from *domination over* to *genuine care for* the inherent dignity of others and of creation itself? We may be more ready than we realize to return to the "radical simplicity" of the reign of God. This radical simplicity may come in ways we had not expected, at a time we would not willingly choose.

In the Beatitudes, Jesus urges his followers to habitually embrace a just and simple way of living—a way of living that is not greed-driven but Gospel-driven. If you want the reign of God, Jesus urges, you have to be poor in spirit. If you want to inherit the land, you have to be meek, and not intent on having it your way and having it now. His teachings run counter to what our culture tells us is the way to make life worthwhile. Yet ultimately, the only truly "new" economy is God's economy, the restoration of God's original simplicity and wholeness in human relationships and culture and in all of creation. We have to "get ourselves back to the garden," as the song goes.[127]

Taking a Prophetic Stance

How does spiritual direction properly and effectively engage your *domestic* conversation? Spiritual direction addresses not only the moral dimensions of your *interior* life, but the moral dimensions of your household decision making—a real and significant starting point for your being in the world. Spiritual direction brings to the domestic conversation the social implications of daily decision making which impact a household's capacity for a prophetic stance in the world.

Standing against the cultural tide and revealing God's view of things through actual choice making and decisive actions can rub neighbors, co-workers, family members, and even fellow church members the wrong way. Such a living witness to a simpler, more reverent, and more equitable way of life can cause people to bristle, sneer, or write you off as marginal, dangerously "radical," naïve, or just plain nutty. Even those closest to you can make you feel like an outsider. The prophetic dimension of your home life—whether expressed or suppressed—is worthy material for spiritual and vocational direction.

Standing prophetically for God's reign of justice, mercy, and peace has always been profoundly, even annoyingly, countercultural, and remains so today. Standing prophetically does not mean pointing a finger of blame—an easy thing to do; rather, it means standing firm against the weight of social and cultural pressure. It means putting your energies and resources at the service of what ennobles and builds up, rather than at the service of what disparages and erodes.

---

[127] Joni Mitchell, "Woodstock" (Siquomb Publishing, n.d.). It is not by chance that the risen Lord, in St. John's Gospel, was mistaken for "the gardener" (see John 20:15), nor even that he rose from death to new life "in the garden" (see 19:41). "Getting back to the garden" in light of the Resurrection means returning to the original grace and goodness of the created order, redeemed and restored in the risen Lord.

Standing prophetically for God's reign of justice, mercy, and peace is precisely the mission and task of the Christ-centered household—your domestic church—where adults, youth, and children alike are most deeply formed in the expressions of authentic Christian life. *Your domestic church is the larger church's living link to the world.* Even if you are a household of one, you are steward of your particular domestic expression of these things that the larger church values and defends.

Each baptized Christian is anointed to share in some particular way in the prophetic work of Jesus himself who spent his short life standing against the tide of the status quo to awaken those who had "ears to hear."[128] And what is this prophetic work for our lives today? What does it mean to live prophetically? It means *to read the signs of the times through the lens of the Gospel, and to act accordingly.* To live prophetically means to be awake—morally awake—to your world, and to actually notice what is going on. Living prophetically requires a willingness to risk the consequences of being morally awake. You risk having your life take a new trajectory, *away from* comfort and self-sufficiency, and *toward* a passion to feel what breaks the heart of God and to press for remedy, justice, and restoration.

Reading the signs of the times through the lens of the Gospel means naming what is unjust and morally unacceptable, even when your voice seems small and ineffective. And the signs of the times today are startling. The recently unemployed and recently homeless are swelling the ranks of the chronically marginalized, the medically indigent, the destitute and desperate, the invisible and voiceless ones. The haunting face of poverty, social isolation, desperation, and fear is everywhere—for those who have eyes to see.

It would be easier to *not* look, to *not* see, but ours are the eyes of Jesus in this world today. It would be easier to tune out, turn off, and simply not hear. But ours are the ears of Jesus in this world today. It would be easier to not feel, but ours is the heart of Jesus in this world today. It would be easier to just walk away, but ours are the feet of Jesus in this world today. *We now* are the ones who

---

128 See Matthew 11:15; 13:9, 15, 16, and 43, and parallels in Mark and Luke.

have been anointed as purveyors of God's mercy and justice, God's love and provision, and God's peace in our time, in this day and age.

It is not easy to be thrust into the role of being socially responsible for the well-being of brothers and sisters whose names you do not know, brothers and sisters who do not look like you, or talk like you, or live like you, or possibly even smell like you. But that is the point of Jesus' most shocking teaching: He identifies with the likes of these nameless ones who seem irreversibly consigned to the margins.[129]

Most of us wrestle with this role of Christ-centered prophetic social responsibility. It can seem thrust upon us like a weighty obligation we should not be forced to bear, a nuisance we would much rather dodge. This interior wrestling with the prophetic nature of our lives and our households is indeed worthy and sobering material for spiritual and vocational direction.

At the Heart of the Christ-centered Household

One outcome of honest conversation concerning your household's moral responsibility to the common good is the nonnegotiable commitments that begin to emerge. Far from easy or convenient, these "nonnegotiables" may challenge you and your household deeply. Naming and actually honoring these nonnegotiables sparks an interior awakening or deeper formation of social conscience in household members. This formation of the social dimension of your family life is the means by which you and your household make a uniquely Christian stand in the world.

In Scripture, Joshua declares his household's unambiguous allegiance to the Lord God amidst a people who were keeping their options open: "Decide today whom you will serve," he says. "As for me and my household, we will serve the Lord" (Joshua 24:15). We may not readily perceive our decision to be a Christ-centered household in such Yes-or-No terms. Many of us "fall into"

---

[129] See Matthew 25:31–46.

Christian life. It is something we inherit and easily take for granted. So it is easy for our Yes or No to become a dispassionate "OK," or even "whatever."

In today's world one can be a cultural Christian and slide beneath the radar of any real commitment. But from a spiritual and vocational standpoint a remarkable difference can exist between the terms "Christian" and "Christ-centered." The difference is a matter of conscious choice, intentionality, firm personal decision, and ongoing commitment. "Cultural" Christian life does not really demand anything of us, certainly nothing that would inconvenience us in any life-changing way.

"Christ-centered," however, means that your conscious, intentional relationship with Jesus, the risen Christ, forms the very core of all that you are and all that you do. This relationship shapes your perceptions, your understanding, your attitudes, and your decision making. The Christ-centered household, like the Christ-centered person, consents to being conformed to Christ,[130] to seek God's willing in all situations, decisions, and actions, and to engage the movement of the Holy Spirit at all times.

The Christ-centered household in fact becomes an *intentional community of mutual caring,* with hearts oriented not only inward in love but also outward in expression of God's goodness, compassion, and justice for others. It would not be uncommon to find that you and your spouse or children may not be spiritually on the same page in terms of understanding your household's nonnegotiable commitments. Or you may discover that the topic of nonnegotiable commitments has never really come up. Honest and candid conversation within spiritual direction can open a pathway for you to guide your household in living a truly Christ-centered domestic life.

Leadership in Your Domestic Church

By and large it is easy to think that the person with the greatest

---

[130] See Romans 8:29.

achievements, the loudest voice, or the most money qualifies as a leader. But history proves that this is not always the case. Moral and spiritual leadership is of a quite different quality. Moral and spiritual leadership comes from a quite different place, and bears quite different results. We can think of the moral and spiritual leadership of a Nelson Mandela, a Mohandas Gandhi, or a Blessed Theresa of Calcutta, a Martin Luther King, Jr., or a Dorothy Day. By God's grace we are surrounded today by saintly and holy models of such powerful moral and spiritual leadership.

What is it about moral and spiritual leadership that sets it apart from mere imposition of power and renders it effective? We can describe it as *authentic* leadership with moral and spiritual roots. It is not coercive or self-seeking; rather, it moves in God's direction, in the direction of highest moral good, justice, equity, mercy, and peace. In St. Matthew's Gospel we read that when Jesus had finished teaching, the people were astonished, "for he taught them as one having authority" (Matthew 7:29). Conversely, *inauthentic* leadership rings hollow. It often is coercive, self-seeking, lacks moral authority, and in truth is no leadership at all.

The authentic leader is a person with a vision and deeply held conviction of a greater *good,* a vision compelling enough to make others want to follow, to sign on, to take action in order to realize that vision. Within the reign of God leaders are collaborators at heart—co-laborers with the Holy Spirit and with others in revealing the reign of God's justice, mercy, and peace.

Bringing this understanding of leadership closer to home, your domestic church, under the hidden yet real leadership of Jesus himself, is both a social structure and an intimate community of persons with a mission to fulfill: *the mission of standing lovingly and effectively in the place of Jesus for the sake of others.* This is not a when-we-feel-like-it mission, or a when-we-have-time-for-it mission, or a when-we-can-be-effective mission, but rather, a mission given uniquely to your domestic church by Christ, by virtue of your anointing. Any restlessness your household may feel to carry out its mission—and hopefully your household *does* feel restless—is the actual stirring of the Holy

Spirit to get moving so that God's reign will be more fully realized in your household and in your world. St. Paul was right—our lives are not our own. God's mission ultimately will be accomplished through each Christ-centered household by virtue of the Holy Spirit who dwells within it.

Small is Beautiful and Countercultural

We have learned, as a nation, and a little too late, that "affordable shopping binges" come at a price. Neither our souls, nor the larger human community, nor our natural environment, can keep up with our unrestrained appetites and our habit of self-indulgence.

Discovering just how much stuff your household has is one way to slow down the frenzy of consumption and return to the gentler ways of the reign of God. *Taking stock* of your household's stuff and curbing the urge to acquire more is a humbling, sobering, intentional act of accountability and self-restraint. A further step—and equally intentional—in the work of restoring balance is the act of *sharing* your excess, rather than storing it, hoarding it, or shifting it from place to place. Sharing your excess is an act of justice and love within the reign of God.

It is difficult today to find a new single-family home with bedrooms, other than the master bedroom, large enough for more than one child and that child's stuff. So we need plenty of bedrooms. With so many ways to spend time in the bathroom, we need plenty of those, too. And with a dizzying excess of cable channels to choose from, family members should probably each have their own TV, so that no one has to fight over programming. The same goes for computers and game gizmos. This may keep peace in the family, but at a staggering social, economic, and environmental price.

And as children graduate up to a driver's license—the young person's ticket to freedom from the constraints of family life—more vehicles are needed. And with the local mall being a primary gathering place for bored and restless youth, we see a cycle of aimless, mindless excess continue on, into the next generation.

Is this culture of aimless, mindless excess what Jesus had in mind for our twenty-first century world? I don't think so. What are the social, economic, and environmental consequences of supersized appetites for more stuff? Jesus would be grieved and rightly angered at our bloated way of living. In fact, he is grieved and angered, in the cries of the marginalized. We should not be surprised when the hopelessly poor of our world—at least those who still possess the physical strength—express the rage and despair of being locked outside the gates of the mansions of plenty. Jesus' parables and beatitudes are as relevant today as in his own time. These countercultural teachings are Jesus' urgent instruction to us today on living life in the simplicity of *God's* economy, not grasping but trusting and thereby creating capacity to receive God's care and provision. God's economy, Jesus insists, reveals the utter perfection of "enough"—a word that means *to supply in such quantity as to fully satisfy.*

Editing down the material excess is necessary and urgent work for Christ-centered households. Because we take Jesus' teachings seriously, we begin to discover that we are both challenged and blessed by the poor who are with us always,[131] who are drawn to us as though we were magnets of God's justice and mercy. In fact, magnets of God's justice and mercy is what God is counting on us to be.

Waking Up from the American Dream

At the turn of the twenty-first century the threshold for buying in to the American dream moved to an all-time high, which seemed not to discourage people, especially those least prepared financially, from strapping ever greater mortgage and credit card debt to their backs.

The American dream always was at best an illusion, a departure from

---

[131] See John 12:7–8.

the alert and responsibly engaged waking state. At worst it has proven to be a nightmare that has led to depression, gambling (financial or existential), and medication (prescribed or otherwise); break-up of marriage, family, and other relationships; deterioration of a sense of personal responsibility and care for the commonweal, and ultimately, a loss of meaningful engagement in life.

In Christian terms, this life of illusion has serious spiritual and vocational consequences. Single-minded pursuit of the American dream leads to abandonment of one's anointing to authentically and wholeheartedly live God's calling. The illusional aspects of the American dream spell vocational stagnation for the individual and, not surprisingly, vocational stagnation within the Christian community. This life of illusion lulls us into a deep vocational comatose state. Participation in the American dream has sealed off many of us from any kind of meaningful encounter with the raw scourge of poverty and from the invitation to encounter the depths of our common humanity—the same humanity which Jesus fully shared.

Who are the poor? Personally, we may not really know (and therefore we may not really come face-to-face with their misery). The poor are no more immune than the rest of us to the lure of the dream, which leads us to ask: What special place does the American dream hold within the reign of God? The American dream has always been about caring for "me and mine," about getting *my* needs met, as well as my wants, impulses, neuroses, and addictions. Others are free to share in the American dream if they can compete with me to acquire the resources that allow them to purchase their piece of the dream.

But competition produces winners and losers, and the reign of God is not about winners and losers. God's dream, unlike the American dream, is about *enough* space, goods, and resources, *enough* housing, education, and health care, *enough* prosperity and economic justice and creative capacity and dignity, beauty, and joy, real joy, for all of us together. The reign of God leaves out no one; rather, it sees to it, even painstakingly, that there is enough for everyone, with enough left over to fill those empty wicker baskets.

Attitudes around pursuit of the American dream—or loss of same, or waking from the American dream and wondering how to embrace God's reality —are all worthy material for spiritual and vocational direction, and all are entry points into the necessary conversation that leads to conversion.

Moving in God's direction requires a careful examination of how you actually live your life in light of the Gospel, and it requires a loving determination to shed what holds you back from moving freely into God's willing for your life and the life of your household.

Bringing It Home

1. What interior conversation am I engaged in regarding the effects of today's economy on my well-being? What questions do I ask? What are my circumstances currently asking of me?

2. Within my household—whether it is a household of one or a household of many, how are purchasing decisions made? What drives my household's spending? How would I describe the conversation around spending?

3. How does my household actually encounter others whose needs demand some kind of humane or compassionate response? How do I (or we) process the tension of inequity and injustice and the cry for mercy and compassion in the face of human suffering?

Hold this Thought

I am finding courage and words to address the discipline of God's economy on my life and the life of my household.

13

EMBRACING THE BEATITUDE LIFE

Who in the World are You?

Was Jesus a revolutionary? A reading of the Gospels leads us to see how he ruffled feathers and challenged the social order, mainly in its oppressive interpretations of the Mosaic law. Many of his parables, in which he seems to both coax and challenge his adversaries, show us the complete absurdity of oppressive systems of governance, commerce, and the social strata in his time. The foolish inequities of his day discomfortingly resonate with our own.

But this is one important thing about Jesus: He was not the center of any revolution. He was not replacing one corrupt social system with another equally corruptible social system. Even at his arrest, when his band of followers was confronted by armed soldiers, he had to be picked out from the others by a betrayer's kiss. Jesus was no revolutionary. Rather, he was the *catalyst for restoration of the original divine social order,* sent on a mission to restore our world from the Land of the Upside Down to the Land of the Rightside Up. Following his execution and burial, the risen Lord was mistaken as one who might be tending the garden. Indeed he was! We are not encountering here any revolutionary but the long awaited Redeemer.

Fast forward to, say, the second decade of the twenty-first century (although any decade of any century would do). Look around you, listen to what's going on, read the news. Has much changed from life in first century Palestine? Not really. Nor should we feel worried. Not because today's injustices and glaring inequities do not matter—they most certainly do. But worry merely undercuts the power of Jesus' instruction to his followers on who they are to be and how they are to act in a world that still stubbornly resists its original loveliness and purpose. Redemption demands a letting go of what is old and a receiving of what is new, a dying and a rising. Redemption demands the hard work of the paschal mystery. Redemption demands our releasing what we falsely cling to for security and protection, in order to receive new life in God who is our justice, our mercy, and, in the midst of ongoing chaos, our enduring peace.

As Christ-centered men and women we acknowledge that the four Gospels, according to Matthew, Mark, Luke, and John, hold a preeminent place in the canon of sacred Scripture precisely because they clearly proclaim the redemptive mission of Jesus' life, death, and resurrection, and speak clearly of this rhythm of dying and rising to new life which distinguishes all of Christian life. Many newly discovered "gospels," usually billed as "sensational" or "shocking," have elbowed their way onto bookshelves usually reserved for serious biblical scholarship. There is a very good reason why these newly discovered accounts of the life of Jesus are not included in the body of sacred Scripture: They lack this distinct and elemental dimension of the dying and rising—the paschal mystery—uniquely expressed in Christian faith.

Jesus' great body of teaching, most extensively presented in Matthew's Gospel (chapters 5 through 7), and including the Beatitudes (5:3–12), holds a unique place within the Gospels. Along with Jesus' teaching in the parable of the Judgment of the Nations (Matthew 25:31–46), the inaugural teachings present the foundation and proper context for the formation of *personal* conscience.

More deeply, these inaugural teachings, along with that culminating parable of the Judgment of the Nations, provide the context for formation of *social* conscience, where a living Christian faith meets the challenge of our common humanity and the world's anguish. These teachings are so challenging, and so contrary to the status quo, that those approaching Baptism—or presenting their infants for Baptism—should be warned: *This life is not for the timid.* Jesus taught us as much in the Beatitudes. We would do well to take a closer look.

The First Beatitude: What is Your Poverty?

Blessed are the poor in spirit, Jesus begins in his inaugural Sermon on the Mount, *for theirs is the kingdom of heaven* (Matthew 5:3). Poverty is what you and I might strive mightily to avoid—certainly financial poverty, but also the poverties that touch every dimension of life: poverty of knowledge, poverty of connections or of opportunities for advancement; poverty of health, or mobility, or independence; poverty of incompetence or inexperience. There is no limit to our human poverties. Not only does Jesus *not* rescue us from this core dimension of the human condition, but he himself embraced it, so that we might embrace it, too, as gift. St. Paul writes: "[F]or your sake [Christ Jesus] became poor although he was rich, so that by his poverty you might become rich" (2 Corinthians 8:9).[132]

A question worthy of conversation in spiritual and vocational direction is this: What *are* your particular poverties? What is your inadequacy? Where do you not measure up? What is gone that you can never restore? What holds you back, or puts you out of the running altogether? These questions—and the honest answers to them—are important not only for directees but for spiritual directors as well.

---

132 The New Testament canticle praising Jesus' selfless offering affirms his willing embrace of the poverty of the human condition: Although "he was in the form of God, / [he] did not regard equality with God / something to be grasped. / Rather, he emptied himself, taking the form of a slave, / coming in human likeness, / ... becoming obedient to death" (Philippians 2:6–8).

You might resist your poverties, curse them, or compensate or deny or try to hide them as imperfections. But if we read the Beatitudes correctly, Jesus sees our particular poverties as a blessing. The poverty itself is simply what it is, resulting from whatever cluster of circumstances, bad choices, or injustices that have visited and shaped our lives. But it's what you do with it interiorly—*in spirit*—that determines the blessing. You can mask your poverty in anger or victimhood or shame, and rail against God for this unearned curse from which you cannot hide. Or you can accept it as a condition that has not escaped God's notice, defend its space, and let it speak to you its inner wisdom and its power to conform you to Christ through a uniquely burnished compassion for your fellow human beings.

Most importantly, Jesus would have us understand, blessed are you when your poverties lead you to a more honest and radical dependence on God. Then, Jesus says, *then* the reign of God is yours—*the reign of God!* Your honest and humble embrace of your particular poverties gives you unexplainable access to the riches of God. Letting go the anger, the shame, the sense of defeat, or feelings of self-pity, is the hard work of conversion. And when you undergo this conversion with all your heart, and all your soul, with all your mind, and with all your strength, you expand your capacity to receive this hidden blessing which is far more precious than any earthly riches.

The Second Beatitude: What in Your World Needs to be Mourned?

When your time comes to journey your way through the land of grief, you may discover something. Honest grieving, real and honest mourning, presents a problem: It means that you have lost something that nothing in the world, and no human being on the planet, can replace. Honest grieving is an obstacle to life as we imagine it should be. It is the irrepressible admission that our world is made of humble clay, not impenetrable steel. Our world indeed is where we pitch our tent, but not permanently, as Peter learned.[133]

Irreversible loss can drive a stake through the human heart. And our culture's remedy of choice to ease the pain of mourning is distraction—through entertainment or food or alcohol or pills, through shopping, a cruise, a "new you." *Good grief,* our world seems to tell us, *get over this dreadful mourning.* The subtext here is easily understood: "You are making the rest of us uncomfortable."

But in this second beatitude, Jesus clearly says, *Blessed are they who mourn, for they will be comforted* (v. 4). Comforted how? With entertainment, a cruise, a "new you"? *Comfort* means to "be with" *(com)* the other, "in strength" *(fortis)*. Comfort is a word denoting relationship. It expresses the willingness to abide faithfully with your own situation of brokenness or loss with a strength that comes not from you nor from the distractions of escape, but from God. But to receive God's comfort and strength, you first have to honestly acknowledge your mourning, embrace it, and enter wholeheartedly into it in order to receive the blessing.

So the critical question here is this: What in *your* world needs to be mourned? What in your inner world, your world of work and vocational engagement, your world of relationships, your world of meaning and hope, needs to be mourned? And what in this complex, terror-driven, anxious and careening twenty-first century world in which you live needs to be mourned? You can watch heartbreaking images on the nightly news, and before your mind can even register the insanity, pain, and injustice of what you have seen, you are bombarded with ads for luxury cars, earth-friendly laundry soap, pills to relieve constipation, and hair products that wash away the gray.

What in your *world* needs to be mourned? Let the question soak in. Allow the human anguish to rise up—perhaps along with unexpected anger, vulnerability, compassion, and the cracking open of the parched crevices of soul

---

[133] See Mark 9:5; Matthew 17:4; and Luke 9:33 for parallel accounts of Peter's desire to set up camp in the glow of Jesus' transfiguration.

where the grace of God's consolation can begin to permeate down into the dry, barren, dark places.

The Third Beatitude: Where are You Pushing too Hard?

"I did it may way" is the title of a song whose lyrics I wish I had never heard. In my waning years I do not want my life's defining phrase ever to reek of such arrogance.

Still, I admit, I am well practiced in an arrogance that renders me unbendable, unteachable, spiritually unformable. My arrogance is a common arrogance, a shared arrogance, a well rehearsed arrogance. Today's arrogance is edgy, enticing, and it's all about "me."

So Jesus' words can ring hollow in our ears as he teaches in the third beatitude, *Blessed are the meek, for they will inherit the land* (v. 5). You, like me, may have no interest in being meek. In fact, upon hearing this beatitude, you may instinctively recoil. "It's not in my personality to be meek," you might say. You may have spent decades overcoming shyness, or you may enjoy a life that has reaped the handsome fruits of your being an assertive presence in the world. And you may discover that like the seed that falls on the footpath,[134] Jesus' words may have no way to effectively take root and grow in your mind, in your imagination, or in your soul.

On first glance, meekness can seem so mousy, so unassertive. Yet by definition a meek person is characterized as gentle, patient, mild of disposition and spirit. True, a meek person can also be seen as overly submissive, spineless, or too quick to acquiesce. What Jesus had in mind in this teaching, I sense, is the person who gives God room to be GOD, the person who honestly prays, *"Thy* will be done," not *"My* will be done." Blessed are the meek, Jesus could have said, because they understand that they are not the moving force within their life. They understand that they are moving *in* God's direction, *at* God's

---

[134] See Matthew 13:1–9; Mark 4:1–9; Luke 8:4–8.

direction.

The helpful question here is: Where in *your* life are you pushing too hard? Where are you bent on making things happen the way you think they need to happen? Where might you be applying the violence of force or coercion? In what circumstance do you beat your head against the wall expecting a better outcome? Where are you bargaining with God, cajoling or coaxing, or worse, giving God an ultimatum? None of these ways of living your life describe the reign of God, the new order, the redeemed life in the Land of the Rightside Up. Blessed are the meek, Jesus tells us; when they let God be GOD, they indeed "will inherit the earth," inherit their rightful place to be.

The Fourth Beatitude: What Injustices Move You to Action?

Today as in centuries past, the church places a value on fasting—as a means of discipline of body, mind, and attitude. Fasting is a way of getting clear of spiritual toxins, a means of calming the soul and body from overstimulation and interior distraction, and coming back to the center, to Christ. When you are free of the overstimulation and the toxins and distractions that pull you off center, you can actually be present to your world in an unobstructed way, and be present to what in your world is going on. For many of us, however, and most of the time, it is easier to live with our more humane and compassionate sensibilities somewhat obscured.

There is a lot of good going on in the world—some of it on a massive scale, much of it quite hidden. But there is a lot of injustice and insidious oppression going on in the world, too. Sometimes the injustice and oppression in the world is too glaring, too overwhelming, more than can be compressed into a two-minute news bite, far more than the human mind can comprehend, and certainly far more than the human soul can bear. It is so easy to pull out the ear buds, switch channels, or withdraw from the news altogether. It is so easy to just get fed up with the endless parade of wrenching human suffering and insanity. And it is so easy to finally become numbed to it all and to lose any capacity to respond or even to care.

In the fourth beatitude Jesus says, *Blessed are they who hunger and thirst for righteousness, for they will be satisfied* (v. 6). The opposite of being "fed up" is "to hunger and thirst," to actually feel the effects of living in a world that resists the blessedness of its God-given beauty. "To hunger and thirst" is to feel the effects of fasting *from* what is false, hurtful, oppressive, or unjust, and to hunger and thirst instead *for* divine restoration of the right and holy ordering of life within the reign of God.

In the Beatitudes Jesus speaks not just about hunger and thirst, but about hunger and thirst *for righteousness*, for the right ordering of relationships and inner spirit according to God's most excellent design. "My food," Jesus tells his disciples, "is to do the will of God."[135] And he says to the multitudes—and to us—"I myself am the bread of life," the food and drink which satisfies this persistent hunger and thirst for righteousness.[136]

Consider these questions: Do *you* hunger and thirst enough for God's righteousness in this world to feel compelled to act when you see injustice? What would it take for you to get hungry and thirsty enough? Or is addressing oppression and working to reverse injustices someone else's concern, or perhaps not so urgent that it cannot be put off a few more years?

The Fifth Beatitude: Whose Suffering is Eased Because of You?

Intractably tied to injustice in the world is the human suffering it causes and the unconscionable stripping away of human dignity—the violation, the rape, of the human spirit. Many of us feel unpowerful—in fact, quite powerless —to address the monumental, systemic, and deeply entrenched injustices in our world. The forces of evil are quite prepared and quite content to keep us feeling

---

[135] See John 4:34.

[136] See John 6:35.

this way. Yet many people resist the narcotic of powerlessness and are stirred to take action to relieve some measure of suffering. Many people do feel impelled to restore to some degree the dignity of those who are caught in the trap of violence and inhumanity.

Blessed are the merciful, Jesus teaches in the fifth beatitude, *for they will be shown mercy* (v. 7). And what is this mercy? At one end of the spectrum, mercy means refraining from harsh measures toward another, holding back from punishment or the exercise of overbearing power over another. And Jesus certainly may have this meaning of mercy in mind. Yet his words signal something more.

In fact, Jesus' reference point in all of his teaching—the true North Star in all of his life—was his Father. Certainly Jesus knew the Hebrew Scriptures, especially the books of the prophets who revealed a God who relents and turns back from unleashing the fury of divine wrath against human stubbornness and sinful practices, ultimately sparing the rod and redeeming the child.

But Jesus understands mercy to be more than merely refraining from punishment. Mercy, ultimately, is the binding up of the other's wounds, relieving the burden of both physical and hidden interior suffering, and restoring the rightful dignity of the one who suffers. The despised Samaritan, Jesus shockingly asserts, is the human embodiment of God who is mercy.[137]

The necessary question here comes down to the particulars of your own life: Whose suffering is eased because of *you?* Is it the out-of-control child who needs your calming adult presence more than harsh measures? Whose suffering is eased because of you? Is it the spouse or parent suffering from dementia and no longer capable of self-care? Is it the death row prisoner who grew up with wounds to psyche and soul that festered inwardly rather than healed? Doing deeds of mercy awakens you to the mercy shown to *you.* Your deeds of mercy awaken you to just how unexplainably tender and personal God really is, and awaken you to these expressions of divine mercy that you might have

---

[137] See Luke 10:29–37.

overlooked or even rejected out of false pride.

The Sixth Beatitude: Where is Purity Expressed in Your Life?

Purity has become something of an old-fashioned word, seemingly not too relevant today, associated as it is with "sexual purity" or *chastity,* another word perceived as quaint and not contributing much to today's culture. Any purity we do find in our world today we sadly assume will soon enough become the inevitable "wrecked loveliness" that all too often overtakes what is young and tender, innocent and full of possibility.

But we find in the Gospels that Jesus places a high value on purity, or being "pure of heart." *Blessed are the pure of heart,* he says in the sixth beatitude, *for they will see God* (v. 8). Jesus is speaking of a morally undistorted way of living. And the gift it brings, he assures us, is astonishing. "Seeing God" seems not so much a reward for good behavior as it is the obvious outcome when you have no impurities or duplicity of heart to block or obscure your vision. By way of simple analogy we could say: Blessed are those with a clean windshield, for they will see the road. Purity of heart is the most direct means to getting a glimpse of God *in this lifetime.*

In our world today, no matter your age, you could find yourself wondering: Is living with a clean heart even possible? Who cares if you stand against the tide and choose to live with a pure heart in an adulterated world? Who cares, indeed, when everyone knows that the swift current will carry you farther?

Purity of heart matters because when you see God, even if only in glimpses, in unexpected and fleeting moments, *you are changed.* Or let me say, you become a little more fully your authentic self-in-God. Interiorly something is awakened, stirred, set more securely in motion toward God. The soul has an unmediated way of recognizing its source, its sustenance, and its destiny. The pure of heart actually cannot resist moving in God's direction. Conversely, the heart that clings to even the traces of impurities cannot see with such piercing clarity, nor can it imagine or muster strength for such an awakening and stirring of the soul toward God.

But even more importantly, purity of heart matters because when you begin to see God, even if only fleetingly, and begin more surely to move toward God, you touch the world in a different and unexpectedly graced way. As a result, your world too begins to change. This graced way of living in the world and touching the world is what it means to participate in Jesus' work of redemption.

So you might ponder these questions: Where is purity expressed in *your* life? Is it sexual purity? Or perhaps it is purity of thought, which is the necessary foundation of a truly nonviolent stance in the world. Or you may find that you are particularly drawn to express purity of attitude, or purity of speech. Perhaps purity is expressed in your life through purity of intention, or purity of motive. What you begin to discover is that purity in one area of your life demands purity of *all* areas of your life.

The Seventh Beatitude: How do Your Expressions of Peace Touch the World?

Peace was not one among many gifts which Jesus gave to his followers. It was the preeminent gift of his resurrection. Not once, not twice, but three times, when the risen Lord appears to the Eleven in the locked upper room,[138] he says distinctly: *Peace be with you.* Above all things, Jesus had proved himself to be the dangerously and victoriously nonviolent One who, with the force of an unshakable interior peace, rattled those who tried hard to rattle him. He underwent his arrest, mock trial, scourging, and crucifixion equipped only with the inviolable peace which came from his "being one with" his Father.

Blessed are the peacemakers, Jesus says in the seventh beatitude, *for they will be called children of God* (v. 9). Jesus was the preeminent "child of

---

138 See John 20:19, 21, 26.

God," the well-beloved Son.[139] Like the Father was the Son—embodying in human flesh divine peace which admits only unity, community, communion, and not the separateness and division which fuel the fires of violence.

Peace indeed is Jesus' preeminent gift, and peacemaking is the preeminent work of those who carry in their hearts the reign of God—rising as it does from the works of forgiveness, reconciliation, and redemption. Yet given its preeminence, Jesus does not place peacemaking first among the Beatitudes but among the last. Why? Well, imagine trying to be a peacemaker if you are haughty (not poor in spirit), unfeeling (not mourning what needs to be mourned), grasping (not meek), callous of spirit (not hungering and thirsting for righteousness), disregarding of human suffering (not merciful), or just plain spiritually polluted (not pure of heart)—all exact opposites of the blessedness that reveals the reign of God.

Peacemaking is not the seed but the actual fruit of a life lived in God. It is not a starting point but a mature way of life tempered by true poverty of spirit, spiritual honesty, humility, and interior pliancy to the Holy Spirit. The way of peacemaking is a mature way of life disciplined by action in the cause of justice and of mercy. People often are instinctively drawn to peacemakers because they are, in human form, the image likeness of God.

These questions are worthy of your reflection: What does *your* peacemaking look like? In what ways do you touch your world with the unshakable peace of the risen Lord? What troubled souls or circumstances in need of peace seem to seek you out? What violence confronting you carries within it the invitation to reveal God's own ways of peace?

The Eighth Beatitude: What Wounds do You Bear for the Sake of the Reign of God?

The first six beatitudes are fine. Many of us can deal with them, find

---

[139] See Matthew 17:5; Mark 9:7; Luke 9:35.

comfort and encouragement in them, and even grow with them. With the seventh beatitude, the one about peacemaking, Jesus seems to put his disciples on a suddenly high-risk trajectory. You can almost hear them silently wonder: Where is he going with this? What is he asking of us—of *us?* Now the proposition of following Jesus becomes uncomfortably self-involving, dangerous, and even costly. If peacemaking can put you in the middle of conflict, the eighth beatitude will turn you unmistakably toward a place you do not want to go.

Blessed, Jesus insists, *are they who are persecuted for the sake of righteousness, for theirs is the kingdom of heaven* (v. 10). And now his language shifts from third person to something unsettlingly direct. *Blessed are you when they insult you and persecute you and utter every kind of evil against you [falsely] because of me* (v. 11). Is this the voice of a madman?[140] Are we to take these words as true and meant for us? *Rejoice,* he says, *and be glad, for your reward will be great in heaven.* Rejoicing in the midst of persecution requires a certain single-hearted, single-minded zeal for the reign of God. And he reminds his followers that the prophets before them received the same treatment (v. 12). Jesus himself eventually will take the prophet's fateful one-way journey to Jerusalem.

Jesus shows us what a wholehearted life-in-God ultimately looks like. For Jesus, lukewarm, half-hearted commitment is no commitment at all. Throughout the remainder of his public ministry he would show us how to live this beatitude, with spiritual integrity, all the way through to his execution and the utterance of his final words. In his arrest and midnight mock trial, in his scourging and crucifixion, he showed us how it's done. He showed us how to undergo this radical surrender to God. He showed us the power of unwillingness to back down from anything less than total commitment to revealing the startling humility, the unsettling meekness, the blazing justice, and brilliant beauty of the reign of God.

---

140 Jesus later in his ministry would be accused by his adversaries of being "possessed and out of his mind" (John 10:20), and by his own family members who "set out to seize him, for they said, 'He is out of his mind'" (Mark 3:20). Jesus indeed was "out of his mind"—out of the place of logic and calculated risk reduction, and "into the heart and the soul" of God's unbounded and foolish redeeming love.

Consider these questions as you ponder the deeper implications of a Christ-centered life: What wounds do *you* bear for the sake of God's reign? At what times in your life have you been roughed up, cut off, dismissed, abused, your reputation maligned, your rights and your dignity stripped away, because you would not back down from what you knew was true and worthy of your standing firm? In what circumstances have you refused to deny God's total and inescapable claim on your life?

What you may have come to discover is that when every support is stripped away, all you have left is the sure abiding presence of the Holy Spirit in the circumstances at hand. When St. Paul realizes that his commitment to the crucified and risen Lord is irreversible and that his own death is imminent, he writes, "From now on, let no one make troubles for me; for I bear the marks of Jesus on my body" (Galatians 6:17). This final beatitude reminds us that there is no such thing as "sort of" identifying with the nail-scarred and risen Lord.

The beatitudes offer real personal challenge as well as real personal blessing. And the challenges on the path to holiness will always be searingly real and intimately personal. Such challenges, often appearing as obstacles, too readily become the "reason" why we cannot fully live the Beatitude life. But Jesus knows just how fragile we can be. The Beatitudes he offers us are powerful encouragements as we undertake the arduous, obstacle-riddled, and self-defining work of moving in God's direction.

EPILOGUE

I wish to add a further word, not only to this book but to a journey I began over a decade ago, the journey into formation as a spiritual director. In a very real way I can say that this journey of formation continues, even though my framed certificate of completion of the course has begun to yellow with age.

To enter into the spiritual directors' formation class I had to write my spiritual autobiography. I say I "had" to write it, because I certainly would not have willingly shared such intimacies of personal memory on my own. But grace prevailed.

On the final page of my eleven-page opus, reflecting on a particularly troubled time for me both professionally and spiritually, I wrote the following words:

> Paschal mystery is an endlessly fascinating subject. Living it is a gut-wrenching journey that rubs against the intuitive urge toward self-preservation.

> My spiritual work at the moment is a dark wrestling between dying to self (and to the urge to protect what I hold to be true) and fleeing a work situation that is very far off center. Where is Christ, I ask

daily, in this place and in this struggle?

And what is gained by my staying here? Yet to leave means, at least for now, leaving a cherished calling perhaps altogether.

I think I have a lot at stake, and then I remember Jesus. He surrendered everything, and trusted that his loss was gain. His hunch proved true: There is no separation from God.

"You could quit your job, move up valley to Salem, and become a sales clerk at Nordstrom," one friend cheerily suggested. "It doesn't pay much, but you could buy fabulous clothes at a discount."

True. Or I could bag groceries at the local supermarket. I could take my 90-words-a-minute skills and join the typing pool. I could sell sunglasses on the street corner. I could become a barista.

But that's not the point. Living, truly and intentionally and willingly living this paschal mystery is a messy, self-emptying process. It is not a game for winners. And it is not a game for losers. In fact, it is not a game at all. It is the work of those who accept that God is big enough and loving enough and merciful enough to be, well, GOD.

APPENDIXES

Appendix 1

THE MECHANICS OF A

SPIRITUAL DIRECTION SESSION

"Do I Just Start Talking?"

Whether you have never experienced a spiritual direction session before, or whether you have been in one or more spiritual direction relationships, you may be wondering: What *should* I expect? How should I prepare? Should I just show up and start talking?

Experience has taught me that a little bit of structure can support great freedom. As spiritual and vocational director I take the initiative to introduce some structure and sense of flow to the session so that the directee knows what to expect, how to be spiritually present and at home in the session, and how to pace the flow of material to be shared. I find that small rituals and a guided process not only give structure to this hour of holy conversation, but set it apart from "just getting together to chat" about what is going on in the life of the directee. Rituals and a guided process make up the "mechanics" of a session while integrating a sense of the sacred into this time of privileged conversation.

Rituals, Processes, and Their Reasons

The practice of rituals, as I use the term here, does not mean becoming "ritualistic" in the sense of excessive or compulsive expression of devotion. Rather, rituals are those actions, words, postures, or other expressions, practiced in a regular way, which set *this* time and *this* holy work apart from the noise and distractions and demands of an otherwise busy day. Rituals allow for expression of reverence.

The "ritual rich" life in the Christian experience celebrates the Incarnational dimensions of one's life, or of the life of the Christian community as a whole. The "ritual rich" life gives intentional and celebratory expression to the living of one's days and weeks and seasons—both personal and liturgical.

Rituals are meant to bring value or to enhance the overall experience in which they are expressed. In the course of the spiritual direction session rituals gently guide the flow of the conversation and assure both the director and the directee that the conversation will not wander aimlessly. The grid below outlines rituals and processes that I have found beneficial to my spiritual and vocational direction practice.

SPIRITUAL DIRECTION RITUALS AND PRACTICES

Before the session	
Process: Review and prayer	Shortly before our scheduled meeting I *review my notes* from earlier sessions. I also *enter into prayer,* to detach from my other activities and to center myself for this conversation and to open my mind, heart, and imagination to the work of the Holy Spirit.
At the opening of the session	
Ritual: Opening greeting of genuine welcome	Whether in person or by phone, the *greeting of genuine welcome* expresses a sense of care for the directee and communicates that I am ready—in heart, mind, and spirit—to engage in our time together.
Ritual: Invitation to silence	When I meet with directees in person, I invite them to *take a seat* in the "directee's" chair. Before small talk can shift the focus, I invite the directee to *take a few deep breaths* to release any interior chatter and to *enter into the silence of our time together.* I use a small chime to clear our hearts and minds of distractions.
Ritual: Greeting of peace	When we have come to a place of interior silence, I gently speak the greeting: *"Peace be with you."* The directee responds with similar words.
Ritual: A small morsel of reading	Next I ask the directee to share a small portion of *Scripture or other meaningful text.* I add: "After you share the reading we can sit silently with it for as long as you would like (usually half a minute or so), and when *you* are ready, we can move to opening prayer."
Ritual: Silence after the reading	The silence after the reading allows the words to soak in, and to orient the two of us to what seems meaningful or spiritually nourishing or spiritually challenging to the directee at this time. The silence also sets the pace for reflective conversation.
Ritual: Opening prayer	Either the directee leads the opening prayer or, at the directee's invitation, I lead it.

During the session	
Process: Opening the conversation	I then may ask: "What is it in this text that most draws you?" (or similar words). Oftentimes the answer will lead the directee to the heart of the conversation.
Process: During the conversation	I give the directee uninterrupted time to say all that needs to be said. During this time I listen, in part, to what the directee is saying. More importantly, I listen to what the Holy Spirit desires me to hear, which may be one phrase spoken early in the conversation, or an incidental comment, or even a particular sigh, that holds the key to what most needs to be examined or explored.
At the close of the session	
Process: Closing the conversation	As the hour comes to a close I may say: "We are coming to the fullness of our time together" (or similar words).
Process: Recap	I may recap any assignments for the directee that have emerged from the session, as well as any actions I will take (such as sending the directee some resource I have referred to). I may point to material we may wish to take up in a future session.
Process: Scheduling	I never presume, but always ask: "Would you *like* to schedule another time to meet?" This question gives the directee a way to set the pace of meetings as well as a way to gracefully step back or take time off, or even terminate the relationship. I need to hear the directee's desire to continue meeting with me.
Process: Taking notes	If I have met with the directee in person, I take a few minutes to recap the essence and any details of the conversation, and to highlight whatever might merit further exploration. (If I have met with the directee by phone, I take notes during the session.)
Between sessions	
Ritual: Daily prayer	I pray for each of my directees, by name, each day in the noon hour.

Appendix 2

KNOWING WHEN TO REVISIT YOUR CALLING

Three Life Conditions Subject to Vocational Shift

We often mistakenly think that a vocation is given once, discerned once, and then you get on with your life in accordance with your calling.

Would that life were so free of nuance and unpredictable change!

I identify three clusters of conditions that occur in the course of life which indicate that a revisit of God's calling and one's most appropriate response is in order. These three clusters include:

1. Circumstantial conditions;
2. Life-work conditions; and
3. Interior conditions.

Circumstantial Conditions

Changes in your *circumstantial conditions* refer to any changes in the circumstances of your life, such as the birth or adoption of a child; loss of a spouse or close family member, especially unexpectedly or prematurely; or the change in your own capacities due to illness or injury. In other words, the big events or major shifts in your life. And while these shifts do not have to be traumatic—for example, marriage or remarriage could be a quite happy change of circumstances—they are situations or conditions that greatly impact the way you live certain—if not all—dimensions of your life, as well as impact your perceptions about your life and the nature of God's calling. These changes in circumstantial conditions can give new shape to your conversation with your interior self, with God, with others, and with your work.

Circumstantial changes may have an additional overlay. For example, the birth or adoption of this particular child may mean the stretching open of your life to welcome a child who has special needs that will never go away, or needs that may demand extraordinary measures toward medical intervention or healing from a damaged past. The loss of *this* particular spouse or family member may come at a time in your life when you are experiencing extraordinary adjustments to circumstances quite apart from the loss.

It may be easy to think to yourself: *Well, this is just what I have to go through,* and press forward courageously. But none of this shift in circumstances occurs apart from God's inscrutable design. This is not to say that a shift in circumstances is *caused* by God's inscrutable design. We have an astonishing capacity to write our own scripts and take our own chances, for ill or for good. God has been known to fashion what is new and lovely from the sharp-edged shards of our unlovely choices.

More than ever, the time when circumstances shift in your life is a time when the objective, wise, and compassionate guidance of a spiritual and vocational director can mean the difference between confusion, discouragement, and bitter retreat, and authentic growth in holiness.

Life-Work Conditions

Changes in your *life-work conditions* refer to any changes in your employment situation, your career path, or the overall trajectory of your life as you live it day-to-day. The shift in conditions here can be subtle, catching up with you perhaps at the point where you discover that your options are not all that open anymore.

Shifts in your life-work conditions can include recognizing patterns of disengagement in work which once energized you, or an inability to stay current in new technologies or to competently handle heavier workloads. You may discover a loss of joy in your work, and perhaps feel unable to name where the spark went or why it went away. You may discover that you have lost sight of the horizon which once held a larger claim on your life, or simply lost an ability to care.

In your life or in your work you may experience insurmountable obstacles to effectiveness, which can range from a loss of self-confidence to an interior—though perhaps unintentional—blocking of the direction your life or your work now need to go. You may discover that in middle age you are now competing with the mental agility and technology skills of a younger generation.

Finally, you may experience soul-weariness or pushback to life's innate invitation to grow to the fullness of your personhood. You may even discover that you have apprenticed yourself to a life of complacency rather than to the discipline necessary for true fruitfulness in your life.

With all of these changes in life and work circumstances it is easy to think that the problem lies with external constraints on your life, rather than recognizing that the challenge and the invitation very well may lie in the core vocational dimensions of your life. An attentive spiritual and vocational director will hear in your words what you may be unable to hear, and assist you in addressing the larger narrative of your life.

Interior Conditions

Finally, changes in *interior conditions* affect the ways you relate to your world—to self, to God, to others, and to the givenness of things as you encounter them. Interior conditions not only *can* shift, but over the course of life we *expect* them to shift. The maturing of the interior self comes with growing pains, rehearsing us into a resilient strength and beauty beyond what could have been revealed at any earlier stage in life.

A shift in interior conditions can include, for example, an unexpected deepening of relationship with the Lord, or a heightened urgency to take this relationship more seriously. Sometimes this shift in relationship comes about in a conversional moment, when you realize how deeply your sins or your transgressions of the past have wounded this most intimate and life-giving relationship. And sometimes this deepening of relationship comes as you mature and awaken to an urgent desire to create or accomplish something that will serve as a legacy for the next generation. Awakening to a greater cause in life, or awakening to the connectedness of your life and actions to the lives and actions of others, can bring a shift in interior conditions. At these times prayer can take on a new urgency, a new depth, a new focus, a new language, the new resonance of a deeper interior self now beginning to speak its truth.

A growing awareness of your own mortality can also cause a shift or an unexpected interior awakening. Such an awakening can come about suddenly, with the diagnosis of a terminal illness. Or it can come about gradually, when you begin to realize that climbing the stairs is a little more difficult, when the joints ache a little longer into the day, when vision or hearing are no longer what they once were. A growing awareness of your mortality can come with the death of a college classmate, a bridge group member, or a long-time neighbor. The sense of loneliness in this interior shift can lead to a withdrawal from life which seems to serve no worthy end, or it can be an indicator that a new and deeper conversation is now ready to begin.

Another interior shift can occur when you experience an awakening of social conscience, or the unexpected expansion of your personal horizon, causing you to embrace the world in a new way. At this point the words of St. Paul may begin to settle in more deeply—that we indeed live no longer for ourselves but for Christ, and for his redemptive mission here on earth. The work of spiritual and vocational direction now becomes a renewed discovery of personal mission and new insight into the trajectory of your life.

Finally, a shift in interior circumstances can come with the honest admission of your innate poverties—not merely the exterior poverties of not having enough money for today's commitments or tomorrow's needs. Here the innate poverties are those existential poverties which visit us all: the poverty of aloneness and even loneliness; the poverty of age and the loss of strength and vitality; the poverty of lost capacities of one sort or another—in short, the inescapable poverties of being human. Awareness of these poverties can tempt you to reject their visitation in your life and to strive mightily to mitigate them. Or, awareness of your innate human poverties can lead you to embrace the totality of your life, and to find peace and strength in knowing that nothing of your life falls outside the love and care of the risen Lord.

The Vocational Piece

For the director, the deeper work of spiritual and vocational direction is to walk the directee through the labyrinth of inescapable shifts in the conditions of one's life, and with wisdom and compassion to lead the directee to the center, which is Christ himself. At no point in life is any one of us free to say, "I have figured out my vocation." To speak such words, or to hold such a thought, is an uninformed and unhelpful arrogance.

For the directee, does this mean that God is capricious in the work of calling you to your fullness of personhood? Not at all. But your life is always in play. Even in your sleep, when you are disengaged from work and relationships and commitments of the daylight hours, your life is in play, and in the hours of nighttime and dream the interior self is still working out the direction and the vision, that wild canvas of possibilities which describe the mystery of *your* life.

God's calling is not "a sure thing" in the way that we like things to be sure. God's calling is seldom perfectly clear. Not because God likes to be difficult, but because at the heart of it all God is holy Mystery, invitation, horizon, yet closer to us than we are to ourselves. The wise and compassionate director makes clear that the directee is a full-share participant in the work of unfolding the mystery, engaging the invitation, and seeking the horizon of the eternal self-in-God.

Appendix 3

SEVEN STEPS IN VOCATIONAL DISCERNMENT

In chapter 9 we explored indicators of mature vocational awareness and obstacles to vocational discernment. But what is the actual vocational discernment process? How do you get to the point in your life where you actually begin to *see or to sense reliable patterns* of God's movement in your life, and begin to *sense the particular trajectory* of your life as you proceed in your return journey to God?

The first step, in a broad sense, is to recognize that vocational discernment is *a process that spans your entire lifetime.* Vocation discernment is an important part of your ongoing partnership with God as you read the ever-changing circumstances of your life.

I propose seven practical steps that can help to guide that discernment process, especially in times when you least think you have anything to discern.

1. *Identify the situation you currently are in or the possible options you are discerning.* You may have just received an academic degree and find that your résumé is light on details. Or you may have lost employment in the economic downturn, with heavy credit card debt and your best productive years behind you. You

may be in your thirties, feeling that the life you live and the work you do is not too bad, but you also are aware of an interior restlessness for something more, and this feeling will not leave you alone. Or you might be like my friend Kathy, happily married and suddenly widowed at age 50. You might lose your high-visibility job like my neighbor did, at age 61, because you no longer project the image the company wants to tout. Many opportunities for vocation discernment in your journey will originate as crisis points which can easily predispose you toward hasty decisions. Take time to calm yourself, gather the facts about your situation, and write down the possibilities and what God might be up to in the circumstances of your life.

2. *Identify where you are right now in the discernment process.* Perhaps you are looking at many options. Or perhaps you feel pressed against the wall. Do you feel an urgency to grab the first offer that comes along? Have you narrowed your field of options, letting go the ones which you already know will drain you of spirit and life? What criteria are you using to identify those few worthy options and to narrow that field? Be very clear in describing these criteria and in stating how they will most likely lead you to the door that God has opened for you.

3. *Identify where you are with your discernment spiritually.* There is a very big difference between feeling quietly guided by the Holy Spirit and feeling gripped in a spiritual panic. Is your discernment of your situation and the options you are facing an expression of trust and spiritual growth? Or is it a cause of anxiety, restlessness, or even hopelessness or depression? What role have you assigned to God—or, how much freedom are you willing to give God—in this discernment process?

4. *Identify how this discernment process shapes your prayer.* When you enter into prayer, notice whether vocational discernment becomes "the problem you take to God" and an excuse for worry. Worry is the soul's unabashed declaration to God: *In this situation*

you are not enough. Worry is a spiritual toxin which must be flushed out of the soul, the mind, the heart, and attitude; flushed out of the mental tapes, the self-talk, and banned from casual conversation. Worry is the language of victimhood, not the language of divine possibility. The antidote to worry is to open yourself unconditionally to the movement of the Holy Spirit and to God's willing. And yes, you can do it.

5. *Identify how your prayer shapes the discernment process.* How you pray and what you pray actually shapes what you experience as possibility and path. The prayer most helpful in the discernment process is a quieting of heart, of soul, of mind, and interior self, as though you were breathing in rhythm with the very breath of God. Notice the ways in which your prayer enables you to find clarity and inner strength to move toward God's willing. Notice the ways in which your prayer offers you clues about what *God* might be up to in your life. Notice any emerging sense of purpose or direction or calling.

6. *Identify the obvious and courageous next steps.* The next step in discerning God's willing in your life might be to research, online or elsewhere, any resources, organizations, or institutions that can offer helpful information or support in your discernment process. The next courageous step might be to follow up on the leads which others have given you. Or the next step might be something simple, practical, and immediate, such as going for a good long walk, or getting out of town for a few days, or reading some poetry, checking in on a neighbor who is homebound or a friend who is ill, or simply doing household chores or preparing a healthy and satisfying meal.

7. *Identify who you want to support you in your discernment process.* Call three to five people who are willing to listen to you, mentor you, encourage you, give you introductions, or point you toward helpful resources. Sitting with a vocational guide, spiritual director, or mentor can give you a way to listen to yourself in the

midst of this vocation discernment process. The conversation also, hopefully, will give you honest and helpful feedback.

Discerning how God is calling you at this time in your life requires your wholehearted involvement. But it is not meant to be solitary work. God does not call you apart from everyone else, but calls you within the context of your human, familial, and ecclesial communities. And God has gifted others to guide and support and encourage you in your vocational discernment process, just as God may be gifting you to guide, support, and encourage someone else.

SCRIPTURE CITATIONS

AND REFERENCES

Old Testament

Genesis

- **3**:9; **18**:1–15; **33**:23–33

Joshua

- **24**:15

1 Samuel

- **3**:1–10

1 Kings

- **19**:12

Psalms

- **16**:11; **118**:19; **119**:105; **131**; **141**:3

Isaiah

- **42**:16; **43**:19; **50**:4; **64**:3

New Testament

Matthew

- **5**–7; **5**:3–12; **6**:6, 31–33; **7**:7;
  11:15, 28–30; **13**:1–9, 15–16,
  43–46; **14**:13, 17–20, 29; **17**:4–5;
  25:31–46; **26**:52

Mark

- **3**:20; **4**:1–9; **6**:31–32; **9**:5, 7;
  12:30

Luke

- **1**:39–45; **6**:39; **8**:4–8; **9**:10, 33,
  35; **10**:29–42; **12**:12; **22**:51

John

- **3**:8; **4**:34; **6**:35; **10**:10, 20, 30;
  12:32; **14**:12, 16; **15**:4–10, 16;
  16:24; **17**:20–24; **18**:11; **19**:41;
  20:19, 21–22, 26

Acts of the Apostles

- **2**:1–4; **8**:26–40; **9**:1–9

Romans

- **8**:26–27, 29, 32; **12**:2

1 Corinthians

- **2**:9; **3**:22–23; **4**:6, 18–19; **6**:19–20; **12**:26; **15**:28

2 Corinthians

- **4**:4–7; **5**:15; **8**:9

Galatians

- **5**:22–23; **6**:17

Ephesians

- **1**:3–10; **4**:13, 30

Philippians

- **2**:6–11; **3**:10

Colossians

- **1**:12–20; **3**:3

Hebrews

- **11**:8–4

Revelation

- **5**:9

BIBLIOGRAPHY

Catechism of the Catholic Church, Second Edition, English Translation. Washington, DC: United States Catholic Conference, 1994, 1997.

Christian Prayer: The Liturgy of the Hours. Psalm texts except Psalm 95 from *The Psalms: A New Translation.* The Grail (England), 1963. New York: Catholic Book Publishing, 1976.

Clarke, John, OCD, trans. *Letters of St. Thérèse of Lisieux, Volume II: 1890–1897.* Washington, DC: ICS, 1988.

Cunningham, Lawrence, ed., with intro. *Thomas Merton: Spiritual Master.* New York: Paulist, 1992.

Ellsberg, Robert. *All Saints: Daily Reflections on Saints, Prophets, and Witnesses for Our Time.* New York: Crossroad, 1997, 2010.

_____, ed. *Dorothy Day: Selected Writings.* Maryknoll, NY: Orbis, 1983, 1992.

Flannery, Austin, OP., gen. ed. *Pastoral Constitution on the Church in the Modern World.*

In *Vatican Council II, Volume 1: The Conciliar and Post Conciliar Documents,* 903–1001. Northport, NY: Costello Publishing, 1975, 1996.

Freeman, Laurence, ed. *John Main: Essential Writings.* Maryknoll, NY: Orbis, 2002, 2004.

Hillesum, Etty. *An Interrupted Life: The Diaries of Etty Hillesum, 1941–1943.* New York: Pantheon, 1983. Cited in Robert Ellsberg, ed., *All Saints: Daily Reflections on Saints, Prophets, and Witnesses for Our Time,* 521-23. New York: Crossroad, 1997, 2010.

Kavanaugh, Killian, OCD, and Rodriguez, Otilio, OCD, translators. *The Collected Works of St. Teresa of Avila, Vol. II.* Washington, DC: ICS, 1980.

Killen, Patricia O'Connell, and John de Beer. *The Art of Theological Reflection.* New York: Crossroad, 1994, 2002.

Merton, Thomas. *Thoughts in Solitude.* In *Thomas Merton, Spiritual Master,* edited with introduction by Lawrence S. Cunningham, 241–250. New York: Paulist, 1992.

Metz, Johannes. *Poverty of Spirit.* Mahwah, NJ: Paulist Press, 1968, 1998.

Michalenko, Sophia, CMGT. *The Life of Faustina Kowalska: The Authorized Biography.* Cincinnati, OH: Servant Books/St. Anthony Messenger Press, 1999.

Moore, Mary Sharon. *Anointed for a Purpose: Confirmed for Life in the Twenty-first Century.* Eugene, OR: Awakening Vocations, 2012.

————. "Listening the Other Into Free Speech." *Presence,* 14:1 (March 2008), 29–33.

_____. *Living in God's Economy: A Practical Guide for Christ-centered Households in Tough Economic Times*. Eugene, OR: Awakening Vocations, 2009.

_____. *Touching the Reign of God: Bringing Theological Reflection to Daily Life*. Eugene, OR: Wipf and Stock, 2009.

Neafsey, John. *A Sacred Voice is Calling: Personal Vocation and Social Conscience*. Maryknoll, NY: Orbis, 2006.

Nemeck, Francis Kelly, OMI, and Marie Theresa Coombs. *Called by God: A Theology of Vocation and Lifelong Commitment*. Eugene, OR: Wipf and Stock, 2001.

_____. *Discerning Vocations to Marriage, Celibacy and Singlehood*. Eugene, OR: Wipf and Stock, 2001.

_____. *The Way of Spiritual Direction*. Collegeville, MN: Michael Glazer/Liturgical Press, 1985.

New American Bible. Grand Rapids, MI: Catholic World Press, 1987.

Nouwen, Henri J. M. *Behold the Beauty of the Lord: Praying with Icons*. Notre Dame, IN: Ave Maria, 1987, 2002.

_____. *The Way of the Heart: Desert Spirituality and Contemporary Ministry*. New York: HarperCollins, 1981.

Okumura, Augustine Ichiro, OCD. *Awakening to Prayer*. Trans. by Theresa Kazue Hiraki and Albert Masaru Yamato. Washington, DC: ICS, 1994.

Pastoral Constitution on the Church in the Modern World. In Flannery, Austin, OP, gen. ed., *Vatican Council II, Volume 1: The Conciliar and Post Conciliar Documents,* 903–1001. Northport, NY: Costello Publishing, 1975, 1996.

Sobrino, Jon, SJ. *The Principle of Mercy: Taking the Crucified People from the Cross.* Maryknoll, NY: Orbis, 1994. In Neafsey John, *A Sacred Voice is Calling,* 146. Maryknoll, NY: Orbis, 2006.

Taft, Robert, SJ. *Liturgy of the Hours in East and West: The Origins of the Divine Office and Its Meaning for Today* (2nd revised ed.) Collegeville, MN: Liturgical Press, 1986, 1993.

Teilhard de Chardin, Pierre, SJ. *The Heart of the Matter.* Trans. René Hague. San Diego: Harcourt, 1978.

West, Christopher. *Theology of the Body for Beginners: A Basic Introduction to Pope John Paul II's Sexual Revolution.* West Chester, PA: Ascension Press, 2004.

Whyte, David. *Crossing the Unknown Sea: Work as a Pilgrimage of Identity.* New York: Riverhead, 2001.

INDEX

American dream, 180–81; as illusion, 189; reign of God and, 190

anointing, 5; as chrismation, 94; as indelible spiritual mark, 59, 63; in Confirmation, 95–150; in domestic church, 187; spiritual awakening and, 13, 20, 38, 120; to be presence of Christ, 65; vocational lifestyle and, 76

Augustine, Saint, 110n66

Baptism: being the presence of Christ and, 59–60; challenge of, 194; charisms and, 5, 22n11; Confirmation and, 5, 111; divinization and, 94; life in Christ and, 13; vocation and, 89, 97, 108, 128; vocational lifestyle and, 76

Beatitudes: as personal challenge and blessing, 206; hunger and thirst for righteousness and, 205–207; Jesus' parables and, 188, 193–94; just and simple living and, 181–82; meekness and, 204–205; mercy and, 207–208; mourning and, 202–204; peacemaking and, 104, 203–204, 210–211; persecution and, 211–212; poverties as blessing and, 195; poverty and, 201–202; purity of heart and, 208–209; thirst for righteousness and, 199

Benedict XVI, 128n82; on importance of spiritual direction, 128

Berrigan, Daniel, 128

calling: discerning vocation and, 129–32, 134; discernment of, 137, 140; living responsibly, 128; ongoing discernment of, 215–16; risk, security, and, 134, 220; vocational awareness and, 138

career: definition of, 10, 65, 113, 129, 162; calling and, 100–101

Catechism of the Catholic Church, 59n31, 80

celibacy: as vocational lifestyle, 80–81, 84–88; vocational discernment and, 109

charisms: definition of, 113; discernment of, 114–15; for celibate life, 84; God's calling and, 111; in spiritual director, 20, 22–24, 26, 44; of Hospitality,

119; of Mercy, 120; of Wisdom, 119–
120

Christian marriage: as vocational norm,
79; definition of, 74, 80;
discernment of vocational
lifestyle and, 85n47; expressions
of, 82; singlehood, celibacy, and,
74, 77; signs for discerning, 80–
81

Christian Prayer, 29n14, 149n103,
167n123

christification: as "becoming in Christ,"
99; as purifying work, 100;
definition of, 94

Confirmation: anointing in, 95–97; as
"conformation," 99; Baptism,
Eucharist, and, 111; features of,
95; in sacramental process, 94;
peacemaking and, 104; three
aspects of, 95; vocational
implications of, 100

conscience, personal: formation of,
194; peacemaking and, 106

conscience, social: as expansion of
personal horizon, 219; as outward
vocational expression, 106;
awakening of, 118; Beatitudes
and, 194; formation of, 117; in
Christian household, 185; in
Matthew's Gospel, 194

Coombs, Marie Theresa, 3, 13nn7, 9,
32n20, 39n24, 74n41, 80–81,
94n51, 111n67, 112n69, 136,
165. *See also* Nemeck, Francis
Kelly

Cunningham, Lawrence, 12n6

Day, Dorothy, 117n76, 150, 186

de Beer, John, 27n12, 172n124. *See
also* Killen, Patricia O'Connell

direction. *See* spiritual and vocational
direction

discernment. *See* vocational
discernment

economy, God's, 182, 188–89

Ellsberg, Robert, 65n36, 115n72,
117n76, 150n105

Faustina, Saint, 39n24

Flannery, Austin, 97n55

Freeman, Laurence, 154n109

fruitfulness: charisms and, 22n11;
compared to "success," 101;
discipline necessary for, 217;
holiness and, 74; in Christ, 37;
patterns of, 87; spiritual, 69, 84,
86, 110; spiritual husbandry and,
36; vocational, 36

Gandhi, Mohandas, 186

Hillesum, Etty, 115n72

holiness, 60–61; Beatitudes and, 206;
fruitfulness and, 74; in marriage,
79; interior urge toward, 27;
journey into, 117; peacemaking
and, 104; personal, 7, 69; prayer
and, 148–49; spiritual clutter and,
139; wholeness and, 35, 120

Holy Trinity, 112n70; icon of, 112;

ABOUT THE AUTHOR

Mary Sharon Moore is founding director of Awakening Vocations, based in Eugene, Oregon, and is an active writer and speaker on the nature of God's calling. Her spiritual and vocational direction practice spans the United States, Canada, and beyond.

Moving in God's Direction is a practical, in-depth resource for those who are, or who are preparing to become, spiritual directors; for men and women receiving spiritual direction; and for all who desire to understand the deeper dimensions of the Christ-centered spiritual journey.

For details on bulk orders or wholesale discounts please call 541.687.2046 (toll-free 1.888.687.2046) Pacific time, or e-mail info@awakeningvocations.com.

Personal and parish resources for spiritual and vocational development can be found at www.awakeningvocations.com. Or call during usual business hours: 541.687.2046 (1.888.687.2046) Pacific time.

Also from Awakening Vocations: *Anointed for a Purpose: Confirmed for Life in the 21st Century*. This personal and parish resource explores Confirmation as a lifelong anointing that enables us to be the living presence of the risen Lord in our place and time. *Anointed for a Purpose* is ideal for young adults and adults of all ages, those who are new to Catholic Christian faith, or for those returning to practice of their faith.

Awakening Vocations

4150 Oak Street | Eugene OR 97405

541.687.2046 | 1.888.687.2046

www.awakeningvocations.com

Made in the USA
Columbia, SC
03 March 2023

13096246R00135